Fun & Original
Children's
Cakes

Fun & Original
Children's Cakes

Maisie Parrish

David and Charles

www.rucraft.co.uk

A DAVID & CHARLES BOOK
Copyright © David & Charles Limited 2010

David & Charles is an F+W Media Inc. company
4700 East Galbraith Road,
Cincinnati, OH 45236

First published in the UK in 2010

Text and designs copyright © Maisie Parrish 2010
Photography copyright © David & Charles 2010

A catalogue record for this book is available from the British Library.

ISBN-13: 978-0-7153-3631-1 paperback
ISBN-10: 0-7153-3631-2 paperback

Printed in China by RR Donnelley
for David & Charles
Brunel House   Newton Abbot   Devon

Commissioning Editor: Jennifer Fox-Proverbs
Project Editor: Ame Verso
Design Manager: Sarah Clark
Designer: Victoria Marks
Production Controller: Bev Richardson
Photographers: Simon Whitmore and Karl Adamson

www.davidandcharles.co.uk

David & Charles publish high quality books on a wide range of
subjects. For more great book ideas visit:
www.rubooks.co.uk

To my grandson William,
for all the joy he brings.

IMPORTANT NOTE
The models in this book were made using
metric measurements. Imperial conversions
have been provided, but the reader is advised
that these are approximate and therefore
significantly less precise than using the metric
measurements given. By means of example,
using metric a quantity of 1g can easily be
measured, whereas the smallest quantity given
in imperial on most modern electric scales
is ⅛oz. The author and publisher cannot
therefore be held responsible for any errors
incurred by using the imperial measurements
in this book and advise the reader to use the
metric equivalents wherever possible.

Contents

Rocking Dragons

Down on the Farm

Butterfly Fairy

Ballerina Mice

Halloween Magic

Christmas Cracker

Cute Christening

Introduction

I am delighted to present the long-awaited follow-up to my last book, *Fun & Original Character Cakes* (D&C, 2009), and I know you are all going to love it! This book focuses on children's cakes, with fun and seasonal projects for you to make and enjoy with your family. Within these pages there are lots of new characters for you to model, bringing real magic and colour to your cake creations.

As in all my books, I have kept the techniques very simple with easy-to-follow step-by-step instructions and beautiful photography for each project. I promise you just can't go wrong! If you are a complete beginner then this is just what you need to give you the confidence to get started, and if you have more experience I am sure you will find many things to get your creative juices flowing.

At the front of the book you will find lots of information regarding tools and equipment, and also a comprehensive section on modelling. Once you learn to place all the body parts in the right places and in the right proportions you will be flying. Facial expressions will give your characters a great deal of personality, and this is something everyone wants to learn more about. As with everything in life it takes a little practice if you want to progress, but the good thing is that modelling is very therapeutic and relaxing, so no matter what else is going on, once you sit in

your own space and apply yourself, you will soon be in touch with your imagination.

Everyone will have their own special favourite among the characters in this book, from the rock-and-rollin' dragons to the ballet-dancing mice, from the whimsical fairy to the mischievous witch, so lets get started and get those modelling fingers moving.

Until the next time, remember ... everything starts with a ball!

Maisie

Sugarpaste

All the models in this book are made using sugarpaste (rolled fondant) in one form or another. This firm, sweet paste is also used to cover cakes and boards. Sugarpaste is very soft and pliable and marks very easily, but for modelling it works best if you add CMC (Tylose) or gum tragacanth to it to bulk it up (see Sugarpaste for Modelling, opposite). This section gives you the lowdown on this wonderful medium, revealing everything you need to know for success with sugarpaste.

Ready-Made Sugarpaste

You can purchase sugarpaste in the most amazing array of colours; just take it out of the packet and away you go. Of all the ready-made pastes on the market, the brand leader is Renshaws Regalice (see Suppliers, page 126), which is available in white and 14 other exciting shades. This paste is easy to work with and is of excellent firm quality.

Tip

Very dark colours, such as black, dark blue and brown, are particularly useful to buy ready-coloured, because if you add enough paste food colouring into white to obtain a strong shade, it will alter the consistency of the paste and make it much more difficult to work with.

Ready-made packaged sugarpaste is quick and convenient to use. Well-known brands are high quality and give consistently good results.

Making Your Own

While the ready-made sugarpaste is excellent, you can, of course, make your own at home. The bonus of this is that you can then tint your paste to any colour you like using edible paste food colour (see page 10). This can then be dusted with edible dust food colour to intensify or soften the shade.

Sugarpaste Recipe

★ 900g (2lb) sifted icing (confectioners') sugar
★ 120ml (8tbsp) liquid glucose
★ 15g (½oz) gelatin
★ 15ml (1tbsp) glycerine
★ 45ml (3tbsp) cold water

1 Sprinkle the gelatin over the cold water and allow to 'sponge'. Place over a bowl of hot water and stir with a wooden spoon until all the gelatin crystals have dissolved. Do not allow the gelatin mixture to boil.

2 Add the glycerine and glucose to the gelatin and stir until melted.

3 Add the liquid mixture to the sifted icing (confectioners') sugar and mix thoroughly until combined.

4 Dust the work surface lightly with icing (confectioners') sugar, then turn out the paste and knead to a soft consistency until smooth and free of cracks.

5 Wrap the sugarpaste completely in cling film or store in an airtight polythene bag. If the paste is too soft and sticky to handle, work in a little more icing (confectioners') sugar.

Quick Sugarpaste Recipe

★ 500g (1lb 1½oz) sifted icing (confectioners') sugar
★ 1 egg white
★ 30ml (2tbsp) liquid glucose

1 Place the egg white and liquid glucose in a clean bowl. Add the icing (confectioners') sugar and mix together with a wooden spoon, then use your hands to bring the mixture into a ball.

2 Follow steps 4 and 5 of the above recipe for kneading and storage.

Sugarpaste is such a versatile modelling medium, it can be used to create an almost endless variety of cute characters.

Sugarpaste for Modelling

To convert sugarpaste into modelling paste, all you need to do is add CMC (Tylose) powder or gum tragacanth (see page 27) to the basic recipe. The quantity needed will vary according to the temperature and humidity of the room, so you may need to experiment to get the right mix depending on the conditions you are working in. As a guide, add roughly 5ml (1tsp) of CMC (Tylose) or gum tragacanth to 225g (8oz) of sugarpaste and knead well. Place inside a polythene bag and allow the CMC/gum to do its work for at least two hours. Knead the paste before use to warm it up with your hands; this will make it more pliable and easier to use.

Throughout this book I have used the combination of sugarpaste and CMC (Tylose) powder, and find it works very well. I personally prefer it to gum tragacanth. If you add too much CMC (Tylose) to the paste it will begin to crack, which is not desirable. Should this happen, add a little white vegetable fat (shortening) to soften it and make it pliable again.

Colouring Sugarpaste

Whether you choose to make your own, or to buy ready-made sugarpaste, the white variety of both forms can be coloured with paste food colourings to provide a wonderful spectrum of colours.

Solid Colours

1 Roll the sugarpaste to be coloured into a smooth ball and run your palm over the top. Take a cocktail stick or toothpick and dip it into the paste food colour. Apply the colour over the surface of the sugarpaste. Do not add too much at first, as you can always add more if required.

2 Dip your finger into some cool boiled water, shaking off any excess and run it over the top of the colour. This will allow the colour to disperse much more quickly into the sugarpaste.

3 Dust the work surface with icing (confectioners') sugar and knead the colour evenly into the paste.

4 The colour will deepen slightly as it stands. If you want to darken it even more, just add more paste colour and knead again.

Marbled Effect

1 Apply the paste food colour to the sugarpaste as directed above, but instead of working it until the colour is evenly dispersed, knead it for a shorter time to give a marbled effect.

2 You can also marble two or more colours into a sausage shape, twist them together and then roll into a ball. Again, do not blend them together too much. Cakes and boards look particularly nice when covered with marbled paste.

Tip

When colouring white sugarpaste, do not use liquid food colour as it will make the paste too sticky.

Edible food colours come in a wide variety of forms – liquid, paste, dust and even pens – all of which can be used to add colour and life to your sugarpaste models.

Painting on Sugarpaste

There are various different ways of painting on to sugarpaste. The most common way is to use paste food colour diluted with some cooled boiled water, or you can use liquid food colours and gels. There are also some food colour pens available, but these tend to work better on harder surfaces. Another way is to dilute dust food colour with clear alcohol; this is particularly useful if you want it to dry quickly. Just wash your paintbrush in clean water when you have finished.

Brushes

In terms of brushes, to paint facial features I use no.00 or 000 sable paintbrushes. The finer and better quality the brush, the better job you will make of it. To dust the cheeks of my figures I use a cosmetics brush, which has a sponge at one end and a brush at the other. For more detailed work, you can use a variety of sable brushes in different widths.

The cheeks of this little girl were dusted with pink dust food colour and a cosmetics brush to give her a nice healthy glow.

Storing Sugarpaste

Sugarpaste will always store best wrapped tightly in a polythene bag, making sure you have removed as much air as possible, and then placed in an airtight container to protect it from atmospheric changes. It should be kept out of the sunlight and away from any humidity, in a cool, dry area at least half a metre (20in) off the ground. If the paste has become too dry to work with, knead in some white vegetable fat (shortening). The main thing to remember with any paste is to keep it dry, cool and sealed from the air, as this will make it dry out and go hard.

Food colour pens can be used to add quick and simple embellishments, such as the freckles on this elf's cheeks. They are cleaner and easier to use than liquid food colours.

Liquid food colour is a great way to add details, such as the markings on this giraffe, which were painted on with a no.00 paintbrush.

Modelling

Mastering modelling with sugarpaste is the key to creating professional-looking cakes. This section reveals all the tools and techniques you need to help sharpen your modelling skills.

General Equipment

There is a myriad of tools on the market for cake decorating and sugarcraft, but many of them are simply unnecessary. The following list gives my recommended essentials, and these are the items that form the basic tool kit listed in each of the projects in this book.

* **Large non-stick rolling pin**

  For rolling out sugarpaste and marzipan.

* **Wooden spacing rods (1)**

  For achieving an even thickness when rolling out sugarpaste – available in various thicknesses.

* **Two cake smoothers with handles (2)**

  For smoothing sugarpaste when covering cakes – use two together for a professional finish.

* **Flower former (3)**

  For placing delicate parts in while working on them so that they do not lose their shape.

* **Paint palette (4)**

  For mixing liquid food colour or dust food colour and clear alcohol in for painting on to sugarpaste.

* **Quality sable paintbrushes (5)**

  For painting on to sugarpaste and for modelling – used mainly for painting facial features and applying edible glue. The end of a paintbrush can be pushed into models to create nostrils, used to curl laces of paste around to make curly tails or hair, and used to open up flower petals.

* **Textured rolling pins (6)**

  For creating decorative patterns in pieces of sugarpaste – for example, rice textured, daisy patterned and ribbed.

* **Pastry brush (7)**

  For painting apricot glaze and clear spirits on to fruit cakes.

* **Cutting wheel (8)**

  For making smooth cuts on long pieces of sugarpaste, for use on borders mainly. A pizza cutter can be used instead.

Plastic marzipan knife

For trimming the edges of cakes and boards for a neat result.

Sugar press (9)

For extruding lengths of paste to make grass, wool, fluff and hair – a standard garlic press, found in all kitchens, is very effective for this.

Plunger cutters (10)

For cutting out different shapes in sugarpaste – such as daisies, hearts, stars and flowers.

Good-quality stainless steel cutters

Round, square, rectangle, butterfly, heart, petal/blossom – in assorted sizes. For cutting out clean shapes for use in decorations.

Frilling tool

For making frills in sugar flower paste pieces – a cocktail stick or toothpick can be used instead.

Cake cards

For placing models on while working on them before transferring them to the cake.

Mini turntable (11)

Useful for placing a cake on so that it can be easily turned around while working on it – not essential.

Measuring cups (12)

For measuring out powders and liquids quickly and cleanly.

Flower stamens (13)

For creating whiskers or antennae on sugarpaste animals and insects.

Non-stick flexi mat

For placing over modelled parts to prevent them from drying out – polythene bags can be used instead.

Cake boards (14)

For giving support to the finished cake – 12mm (½in) thickness is ideal.

Specific Modelling Tools

A whole book could be filled talking about these, as there are so many different varieties available. However, I use the white plastic set that has a number on each tool. I refer to the number on the tool throughout the book. They are inexpensive, light and easy to work with, and are available to buy from my website (see Suppliers, page 126).

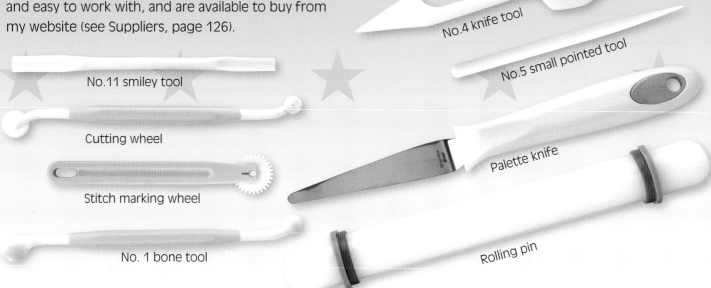

No.12 stitch marking tool

No.3 tapered cone/ball tool

No.4 knife tool

No.5 small pointed tool

No.11 smiley tool

Cutting wheel

Stitch marking wheel

Palette knife

No. 1 bone tool

Rolling pin

Securing and Supporting Your Models

Sugarpaste models need to be held together in several ways. Small parts can be attached with edible glue (see page 26), but larger parts, such as heads and arms, will require additional support.

Throughout the book I use pieces of dry spaghetti for this purpose. The spaghetti is inserted into the models – into the hip, shoulder or body, for example – on to which you can attach another piece – the leg, arm or head. Leave 2cm (¾in) showing at the top to support the head, and 1cm (⅜in) to support arms and legs.

The pieces will still require some edible glue to bond them, but will have more support and will stay rigid. When inserting spaghetti to support heads, make sure that it is pushed into the body in a very vertical position otherwise the head will tilt backwards and become vulnerable.

I recommend using dry spaghetti because it is food and is much safer than using cocktail sticks or toothpicks, which could cause harm, particularly to children. However, I would always advise that the spaghetti is removed before eating the cake and decorations.

Sugarpaste models sometimes need to be supported with foam or cardboard while they are drying to prevent parts from flopping over or drooping down. Advice on where this may be necessary is given in the project instructions.

Basic Shapes

There are four basic shapes required for modelling. Every character in this book begins with a ball; this shape must be rolled first, regardless of whatever shape you are trying to make.

Ball

The first step is always to roll a ball. We do this to ensure that we have a perfectly smooth surface, with no cracks or creases.

For example:
If you pull out the ball at the front, you can shape it into an animal's face.

Sausage

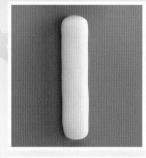

From this shape we can make arms and legs. It is simple to make by applying even pressure to the ball and continuing to roll, keeping it uniform thickness along its length.

For example:
The sausage shape when turned up at the end will form a foot, or can be marked to make a paw.

Cone

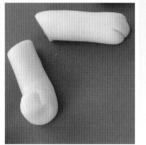

This shape is the basis for all bodies. It is made by rolling and narrowing the ball at one end, leaving it fatter at the other.

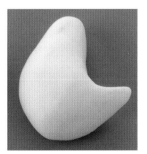

For example:
The cone can be pulled out at the widest part to form the body of a bird.

Oval

This is the least used of the basic shapes, but is used to make cheeks, ears and other small parts. It is made in the same way as the sausage, by applying even pressure to the ball, but not taking it as far.

For example:
Smaller oval shapes can be used for ears.

How to Give Your Characters Personality

When you start to model a character start as if you have a blank piece of paper, and, just like an artist, begin to form the basic shapes. On top of these, then add the details that will eventually become the character you have in mind.

The Head Shape

There are many different head shapes. If you think about it, this is one of the things that gives us our character. Decide what the personality of the character is going to be, and then go ahead and create it. It is the details you put on to the shape that will determine the finished character.

The heads shown on the right are made from a simple shape, and all the elements are then added to create the finished appearance.

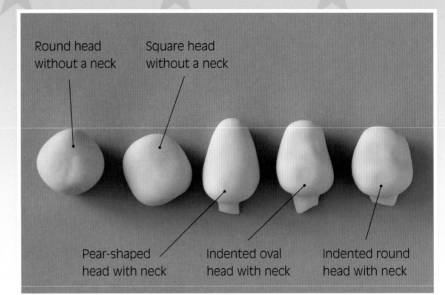

Round head without a neck

Square head without a neck

Pear-shaped head with neck

Indented oval head with neck

Indented round head with neck

How to Construct a Head

In this quick step-by-step example, I will show you how to make a baby's head.

1 Start by rolling a basic ball shape (see page 15). Place the ball into the palm of your hand, and with the side of your little finger on the opposite hand, lightly indent the eye area by rocking it backwards and forwards (**A**).

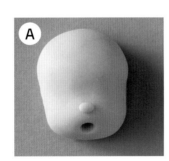

2 Roll a tiny oval shape for the nose and attach to the centre of the face with edible glue (**A**).

3 Push the end of your paintbrush into the mouth area, pulling it down to make a simple but effective mouth (**A**).

4 Roll two small balls for the ears and attach to the side of the face. Push the end of your paintbrush into the balls to indent them. The ears should look rounded and low set (**B**).

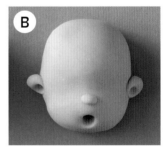

5 Make two flattened white oval shapes for the eyes, which will look much cuter if they are large, and glue to the face above and on either side of the nose (**C**).

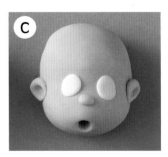

6 Add two smaller flattened oval shapes in a lighter shade of blue on top, leaving some whites of the eyes showing. On top of these, add two smaller flattened ovals in a darker shade for pupils (**D**).

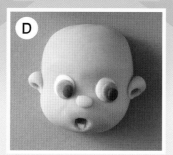

7 Attach a tiny piece of white inside the mouth opening for some bottom teeth (**D**).

8 Emphasize the eyes by painting a fine line of liquid food colour in a darker shade of blue around the edge of the pale blue shape (**E**).

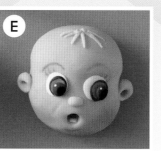

9 Dip the end of a cocktail stick into some white paste food colour or edible paint and use this to add a highlight to each eye (**E**).

10 Dust the cheeks with pale pink dust food colour and a dry brush. Using a No.0000 paintbrush make a fine arched eyebrow using a light brown liquid food colour, and then add some fine eyelashes (**E**).

11 Roll three or four thin tapered cone shapes and glue to the top of the head for the hair (**E**).

Tip

Use a flower former to hold the head in shape while you are working on it.

Faces

To construct any face, such as the ones shown here, use the same order as for the baby in the step-by-step example. First, form the basic shape, then add the nose, the ears, the mouth and the eyes. Finish off with the hair.

Wide-eyed happy expression

Blonde hair in a neat style

Cute button nose

Rounded pink cheeks

Wide smile reveals teeth

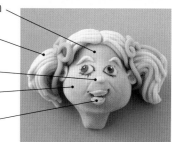

Expression of a very spoiled child

Crying with eyes tightly shut

Tears flowing down cheeks

Wide open mouth

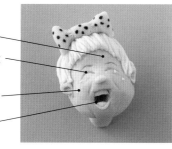

Pear-shaped face

Large eyes

Ears set low

Freckles and dimples give him an innocent look

Smile shows two teeth

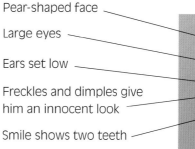

Comical, dopey expression

Unkempt hair

Eyes are small and close set

Ears are low set and round

Large upper lip hides teeth

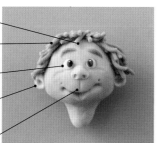

Black hair tipped with colour

Large brown eyes

A happy face with a nicely rounded shape

Full lips

Teeth are large and very white

Hairstyles

Hair is a great way of adding personality to your characters. For this example I will show you how to make a simple girl's hairstyle.

1 Fill the cup of a sugar press (or garlic press) with the desired colour of sugarpaste mixed with some white vegetable fat (shortening) and extrude the hair. Do not chop the hair off in a clump, but slide tool no.4 through a few strands, taking off a single layer at a time.

2 Apply edible glue around the head, and then starting at the back of the head, work around the sides adding thin layers of hair. If there is a parting at the back of the head, work from the parting to the side of the head, keeping in mind the direction in which you would comb the hair.

3 To make bunches, extrude the hair and cut off several strands together, forming a bunch. Attach to the side of the head and shape as desired.

4 If you want ringlets, take three strands of hair and twist them together, make three for each side of the head and arrange them together. Add a ribbon to finish by rolling a small white sausage shape.

Head and Body Shapes

As you can see from the image shown below, if a body has no neck, then the neck will be modelled with the head, and likewise, if the head has a neck, then the body will be modelled without one.

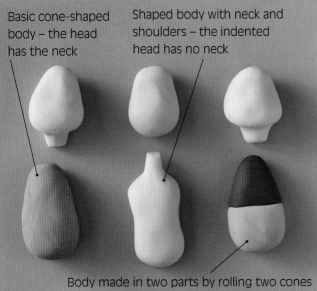

Basic cone-shaped body – the head has the neck

Shaped body with neck and shoulders – the indented head has no neck

Body made in two parts by rolling two cones in different colours. Cut both cones in half and attach the top of one to the base of the other. The head for this body has a neck

Hands and Feet

When making an arm, first roll a sausage with rounded ends. Narrow the wrist area by rolling it gently, and then narrow just above the elbow. Make a diagonal cut at the top of the arm to fit the body shape. Flatten the hand end to look like a wooden spoon.

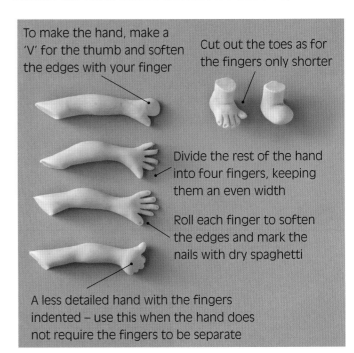

To make the hand, make a 'V' for the thumb and soften the edges with your finger

Cut out the toes as for the fingers only shorter

Divide the rest of the hand into four fingers, keeping them an even width

Roll each finger to soften the edges and mark the nails with dry spaghetti

A less detailed hand with the fingers indented – use this when the hand does not require the fingers to be separate

Making Clothes

How you dress your characters is the final statement of their personality. Here I will show you how to make a pair of dungarees and a dress, both of which are very simple. With any clothing, you have to tailor it to the size of the body you are dressing, making sure the garments fit from side to side and from top to bottom.

Front of garment – trouser section and bib. Pockets with stitch marks add interest

Back of garment – trouser section and braces. Patches add colour and fun

Front of garment – square neck with a double frill and ribbon decoration

Back of garment – high cut with a button opening. You could also add sleeves

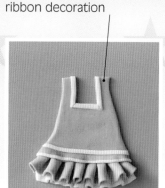

Shoes and Hats

Accessories such as hats and shoes are great fun to make. It is these little finishing touches that add to the charm of your finished character. Now you have lots of inspiration to create your own characters with bags of personality!

Girl's red shoe with separate sole, strap, button detail and socks – use dry spaghetti to attach directly to end of leg

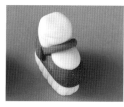

Pink slipper with pretty white bow – inside hollowed out with tool no.1 for the leg to be slipped inside

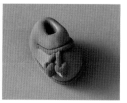

Blue boot with red heart tie – the top is hollowed out just wide enough to fit the leg

Black and white sports shoe with tongue and laces – again, inside hollowed out so the leg can sit inside

Bobble hat – formed from a cone of sugarpaste hollowed out with fingers to fit the head. Decorated with bands, stripes and furry bobbles extruded through a sugar press (or garlic press)

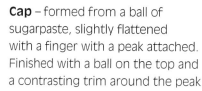

Cap – formed from a ball of sugarpaste, slightly flattened with a finger with a peak attached. Finished with a ball on the top and a contrasting trim around the peak

Sun hat – made by mixing three or four different shades together to form a ball and flattening the top with a finger. A circle was cut out for the brim and attached to the head

Creating Animal Characters

Using the basic shapes as a starting point (see page 15), you can create a vast selection of different animals full of personality and charm. Each project gives detailed instructions for creating the featured characters, but here is a sample of some additional animals with advice on how to model them. Use these examples to practise and hone your modelling skills before you launch into the cake projects.

Mouse

Mice are well known for causing trouble and can be great characters to have on a cake. They come in many sizes and shapes, but all have shared characteristics. The shorter the nose the cuter the mouse will look; if it gets too long it will start to look more like a rat. Three basic shapes are needed: ball, cone and oval.

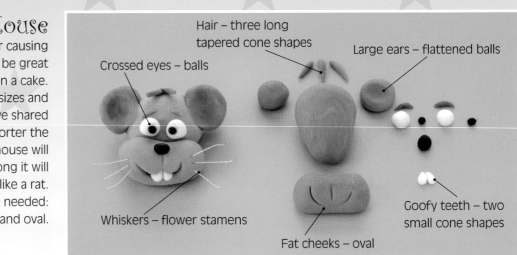

Hair – three long tapered cone shapes

Crossed eyes – balls

Large ears – flattened balls

Whiskers – flower stamens

Fat cheeks – oval

Goofy teeth – two small cone shapes

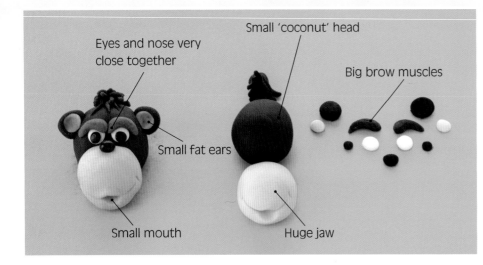

Small 'coconut' head

Eyes and nose very close together

Big brow muscles

Small fat ears

Small mouth

Huge jaw

Monkey

This cheeky money is almost the same as the mouse, but we make him with balls of different sizes. His tuft of hair at the top makes him look really cute. He can be made using eight balls and sausage shapes for the eyebrows.

Lion

The lion is, of course, the King of the jungle, but my lion has such a sweet innocent look, he couldn't harm anyone. He is made from six balls, plus one large and one small cone shape.

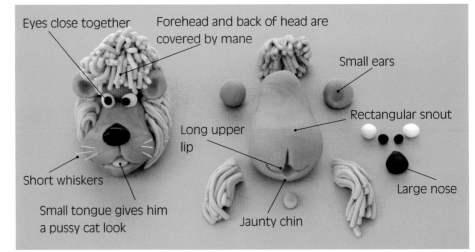

Eyes close together

Forehead and back of head are covered by mane

Small ears

Short whiskers

Small tongue gives him a pussy cat look

Long upper lip

Jaunty chin

Rectangular snout

Large nose

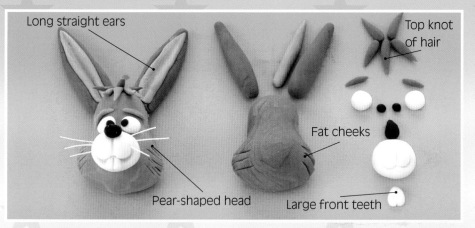

Long straight ears

Top knot of hair

Fat cheeks

Pear-shaped head

Large front teeth

Rabbit

This happy-go-lucky countryside resident is always ready for his next meal. He is full of character with his cross-eyed look and long ears. His eyes are close together and he has a distinctive goofy smile. He is made using eight cone shapes, five balls and four ovals.

Elephant

Every part of this huge animal is thick, fat and round. You could give him all sorts of expressions but this one is my favourite. The head is formed from a large cone, and then you pull out the trunk and continue to shape the face. The ears are made from oval shapes.

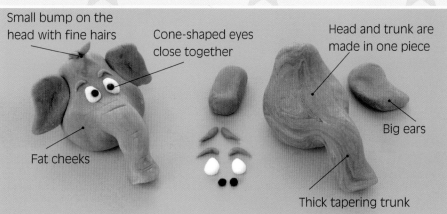

Small bump on the head with fine hairs

Cone-shaped eyes close together

Head and trunk are made in one piece

Big ears

Fat cheeks

Thick tapering trunk

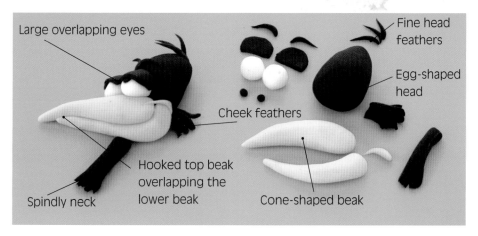

Large overlapping eyes

Fine head feathers

Egg-shaped head

Cheek feathers

Hooked top beak overlapping the lower beak

Cone-shaped beak

Spindly neck

Crow

What a classic cartoon character this bird is. The construction of the head is very simple, using three cone shapes, two circles and four balls, plus a few feathers.

Dog

I couldn't complete a book without including my favourite Old English sheepdog. He never fails to enchant, with a simple tussled head that makes him irresistible. He is made using a cone shape for the head, flattened at the front, and simply covered in a sunburst of tapered cone shapes.

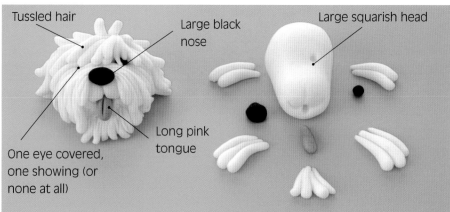

Tussled hair

Large black nose

Large squarish head

Long pink tongue

One eye covered, one showing (or none at all)

 Cake Recipes

Before you can get on to the business of decorating your cake, first you need to bake it! While there are thousands of books on cake making for you to refer to, here are my tried-and-tested recipes for both sponge and fruit cakes and for the small cakes that you will find at the end of every project.

Madeira Cake

This is a very nice firm cake that will keep for up to two weeks, giving you plenty of time to decorate it. It can also be frozen. I use it because if you are placing sugarpaste characters on the top it stays firm and will not sink. The recipe here is for a plain cake, but you can flavour both the sponge and the buttercream (see page 26) to suit your own taste.

Ingredients

For a 20cm (8in) round cake

- ✱ 115g (4oz) plain flour
- ✱ 225g (8oz) self-raising flour
- ✱ 225g (8oz) butter (at room temperature)
- ✱ 225g (8oz) caster sugar
- ✱ 4 eggs

Method

1 Pre-heat the oven to 160ºC (320ºF, Gas Mark 3). Grease the tin and line with greaseproof paper, then grease the paper as well.

2 Sift the flours into a large mixing bowl and add the butter and sugar. Beat together until the mixture is pale and smooth. Add the eggs and beat well, adding more flour if the mixture becomes too loose.

3 Spoon the mixture into the tin, and then make a dip in the top with the back of a spoon to prevent the cake from rising too much.

4 Bake in the centre of the oven for 1–1¼ hours. Test the cake (see tip opposite) and when it is cooked, remove it from the oven and leave it to stand in the tin for about 5 minutes, then turn it out on to a wire rack to cool fully.

5 Cover the cake around the sides and top with a coating of buttercream (see page 26), then cover with rolled sugarpaste (see page 28).

Tip

The temperatures stated and baking times given are for fan-assisted ovens, which is what I use. If you are using a conventional oven, you will need to adjust the timings accordingly.

Rich Fruit Cake

This delicious cake improves with time, so always store it away before decorating it. I find it is generally at its best four weeks after baking, provided it is stored properly and fed with a little extra brandy!

Ingredients

For a 20cm (8in) cake

- ★ 575g (1lb 4¼oz) currants
- ★ 225g (8oz) sultanas
- ★ 85g (3oz) glacé cherries
- ★ 85g (3oz) mixed peel
- ★ 60ml (4tbsp) brandy
- ★ 285g (10oz) plain flour
- ★ 2.5ml (½tsp) salt
- ★ 1.25ml (¼tsp) nutmeg
- ★ 3.75ml (¾tsp) mixed spice
- ★ 285g (10oz) dark soft brown sugar
- ★ 285g (10oz) butter (at room temperature)
- ★ 5 eggs
- ★ 85g (3oz) chopped almonds
- ★ Grated zest of 1 orange and 1 lemon
- ★ 15ml (1tbsp) black treacle

Tip

Test whether a cake is ready by inserting a fine cake skewer into the centre. If the cake is ready, the skewer will come out clean, if not, replace the cake for a few more minutes and then test it again.

Method

1 Place all the fruit and peel into a bowl and mix in the brandy. Cover the bowl with a cloth and leave to soak for 24 hours.

2 Pre-heat the oven to 140°C (275°F, Gas Mark 1). Grease the tin and line with greaseproof paper, then grease the paper as well.

3 Sieve the flour, salt and spices into a mixing bowl. In a separate bowl, cream the butter and sugar together until the mixture is light and fluffy.

4 Beat the eggs and then add a little at a time to the creamed butter and sugar, beating well after each addition. If the mixture looks as though it is going to curdle, add a little flour.

5 When all the eggs have been added, fold in the flour and spices. Then stir in the soaked fruit and peel, the chopped almonds, treacle and the grated orange and lemon zest.

6 Spoon the mixture into the prepared tin and spread it out evenly with the back of a spoon.

7 Tie some cardboard or brown paper around the outside of the tin to prevent the cake from overcooking on the outside before the inside is done, then cover the top with a double thickness of greaseproof paper with a small hole in the centre to let any steam escape.

8 Bake the cake on the lower shelf of the oven for 4¼–4¾ hours. Do not look at the cake until at least 4 hours have passed, then test it (see tip above left).

9 When cooked, remove from the oven and allow to cool in the tin. When quite cold, remove from the tin but leave the greaseproof paper on as this helps to keep the cake moist. Turn the cake upside down and wrap in more greaseproof paper, then loosely in polythene and store in an airtight tin. Store in a cool, dry place.

10 You can feed the cake with brandy during the storage time. To do this, make a few holes in the surface of the cake with a fine skewer and sprinkle a few drops of brandy on to the surface. Reseal and store as above. Do not do this too often though or you will make the cake soggy.

11 Glaze the cake with apricot glaze (see page 27), then cover with rolled marzipan and sugarpaste (see pages 28–30).

Mini Cakes

These charming mini cakes are very popular and make the main cake go much further. Children love them, especially if they are made from sponge, which you can flavour to your personal taste. Ideally, use the Silverwood 5cm (2in) multi-mini pan set (see Suppliers, page 126), but if you don't have this you can just make one large cake and cut it into individual squares. Serve the cakes on 7.5cm (3in) cake cards.

Ingredients

For 16 mini cakes or one 18cm (7in) cake to be cut into squares

★ 250g (8¾oz) self-raising flour
★ 250g (8¾oz) caster sugar
★ 250g (8¾oz) butter (at room temperature)
★ 4 eggs

Method

1 Pre-heat the oven to 180ºC (350ºF, Gas Mark 4), and prepare the cake pans with silicone liners or with greaseproof paper.

2 Prepare the mixture as for the Madeira cake (see page 22) and half fill each cake pan. Bake in the centre of the oven for 15–20 minutes. You may wish to put a baking sheet on the bottom shelf to catch any drips. When cooked, remove from the oven and allow to cool to room temperature.

3 For perfect cubes, leave the cooled cakes in the pans and slice neatly across the tops with a long-bladed knife, using the pan tops as a cutting guide.

4 Remove the pans from the base and gently pull the halves apart to remove the cakes. You may need to run a thin-bladed knife around the top edges to release any slight overspill. Place the cakes on a wire rack. Once cooled, keep them covered, as they will dry out very quickly.

5 Cover each cake around the sides and top with a coating of buttercream (see page 26), then cover with rolled sugarpaste (see pages 28–29).

Cup Cakes

An alternative to the mini cakes is to use good old-fashioned cup cakes, which are simple to make and just as delicious. They can be iced with a simple circle of sugarpaste then decorated as desired.

Ingredients

For 12 cup cakes

★ 175g (6oz) butter (at room temperature)
★ 175g (6oz) golden caster sugar
★ Finely grated zest of 1 orange
★ 2 large eggs
★ 100ml (7tbsp) milk
★ 175g (6oz) plain flour
★ 7.5ml (1½tsp) baking powder

Method

1 Pre-heat the oven to 180ºC (350ºF, Gas Mark 4).

2 Place all the ingredients into a food processor and cream together.

3 Arrange the paper cases inside two fairy cake tins and spoon the mixture into them, filling them two-thirds full.

4 Bake for 15 minutes until risen and springy to the touch, then remove from the oven and leave to cool.

5 Ice and decorate as desired.

Other Recipes

Now you have your sugarpaste (see pages 8–9) and your cakes (see pages 22–24) ready and waiting, there are a few other recipes you will need in order to complete the projects in this book.

Sugar Flower Paste

This is a good strong paste that can be rolled very thinly. It is ideal for making delicate objects such as butterflies and stars (see pages 61 and 113 for examples). The best sugar flower paste is bought ready-made, but you can make your own from the following recipe.

The exquisite butterflies on the Butterfly Fairy cake (see pages 58–71) were made using sugar flower paste, which can be rolled out very thinly and dries super hard so that the wings don't flop down.

Ingredients

★ 25ml (5tsp) cold water
★ 10ml (2tsp) powdered gelatin
★ 500g (1lb 1½oz) icing (confectioners') sugar
★ 10ml (2tsp) liquid glucose
★ 15ml (1tbsp) gum tragacanth
★ 15ml (3tsp) white vegetable fat (shortening)
★ 1 egg white (or the equivalent made up from dried egg albumen)

Method

1 Place the water in a small heatproof bowl. Sprinkle the gelatin over the water and leave to soak for around 30 minutes until it becomes spongy.

2 Stand the bowl over a pan of hot water and stir until dissolved. Add the glucose and white vegetable fat (shortening) to the gelatin, and continue to heat and stir until all the ingredients have melted and mixed together.

3 Carefully sift the icing (confectioners') sugar and gum tragacanth into the bowl of an electric mixer and fit the bowl to the machine.

4 Add the gelatin mixture to the icing (confectioners') sugar then add the egg white. Turn the mixer on at its lowest speed. Beat until mixed and then increase the speed to maximum and continue beating until the paste is white and stringy.

5 Empty the paste out, then roll tightly in a polythene bag. Store it in an airtight container until required. It will keep for several weeks if stored correctly.

Edible Glue

This is the glue that holds sugarpaste pieces together, used in every project in this book. Always make sure your glue is edible before applying it to your cake.

> **Tip**
>
> Should you require stronger glue, use gum tragacanth as the base. Mix 5ml (1tsp) gum tragacanth powder with a few drops of water to make a thick paste. Store in an airtight container in the fridge.

Ingredients

★ 1.25ml (¼tsp) CMC (Tylose) powder
★ 30ml (2tbsp) boiled water, still warm
★ A few drops of white vinegar

Method

1 Mix the CMC (Tylose) powder with the warm boiled water and leave it to stand until the powder has fully dissolved. The glue should be smooth and to a dropping consistency. If the glue thickens after a few days, add a few more drops of warm water.

2 To prevent contamination or mould, add a few drops of white vinegar.

3 Store the glue in an airtight container in the fridge and use within one week.

Buttercream

A generous coating of buttercream precedes the covering of sugarpaste on all sponge cakes. The classic version is flavoured with a few drops of vanilla essence, but you could substitute this for cocoa powder or grated lemon/orange zest to suit your particular taste.

Sweet and delicious, buttercream is simple to make and is the ideal covering for both large and mini sponge cakes. Smooth on a generous layer with a palette knife before they are covered in sugarpaste.

Ingredients

To make 480g (1lb) of buttercream

★ 110g (4oz) butter (at room temperature)
★ 30ml (2tbsp) milk
★ 350g (12oz) sifted icing (confectioners') sugar

Method

1 Place the butter into a mixing bowl and add the milk and any flavouring required.

2 Sift the icing (confectioners') sugar into the bowl a little at a time. Beat it after each addition until all the sugar has been incorporated. The buttercream should be light and creamy in texture.

3 Store in an airtight container for no more than one week.

Gum tragacanth, CMC (Tylose) powder, apricot glaze and confectioners' glaze are essential products that you will need to purchase before you begin sugarcrafting (see Suppliers, page 126).

Essential Purchases

A visit to your local cake decorating or sugarcraft shop is a must – not only can you buy all the necessary products there, you will also come away very inspired! These products cannot be made at home with any great ease, and therefore need to be purchased.

✷ Gum tragacanth

This is a natural gum, which comes in the form of fine white powder used for thickening and strengthening sugarpaste for modelling (see page 9).

✷ CMC (Tylose) powder

Carboxymethylcellulose is a synthetic and less expensive substitute for gum tragacanth. It is used as a thickening agent when added to sugarpaste, and also used for edible glue.

✷ Apricot glaze

This glaze is painted on to fruit cakes before adding a layer of marzipan (see page 30). It is made from apricot jam, water and lemon juice, which is boiled then sieved. Although it would be possible to make your own, I don't know anyone who does, as it is so easy to use straight from the jar.

✷ Confectioners' glaze

This product is used to highlight the eyes, shoes, or anything you want to shine on your model. It is particularly useful if you want to photograph your cake, as it will really add sparkle. Apply a thin coat and let it dry, then apply a second and even a third to give a really deep shine. It is best kept in a small bottle with brush on the lid – this way the brush is submerged in the glaze and doesn't go hard. If you use your paintbrush to apply it, then you will have to clean it with special glaze cleaner.

Covering Cakes

Most beginners can successfully cover a cake with sugarpaste. However, a professional finish – a glossy surface free of cracks and air bubbles with smooth rounded corners – will only result from practise.

1 Prepare the cake with a layer of buttercream (see page 26) or apricot glaze and marzipan (see page 30) depending on whether it is a sponge or a fruit cake.

2 Take sufficient sugarpaste to cover the complete cake. The quantity required for each of the cakes in this book is given at the start of each project. Work the paste until it is quite soft and smooth, then place it on to a surface lightly dusted with icing (confectioners') sugar.

3 Roll out the paste with a non-stick rolling pin – spacing rods can be used to maintain a uniform thickness (**A**). The depth of the paste should be approximately 4mm (⅛in). As you roll the paste, move it regularly to ensure it has not stuck to the surface.

4 Measure the cake by taking a measuring tape up one side, over the top and down the other side. The sugarpaste should be rolled out in the shape of the cake to be covered (round for a round cake, square for a square cake and so on), and rolled out a little larger than the measurement just made.

Tip

When covering a cake, try to do it in natural daylight, as artificial light makes it more difficult to see flaws. Sometimes imperfections can be covered, but sometimes they will occur where you are not going to put decorations so you need to strive for a perfect finish every time. However, if things don't go to plan, don't worry; the sugarpaste can be removed and re-applied.

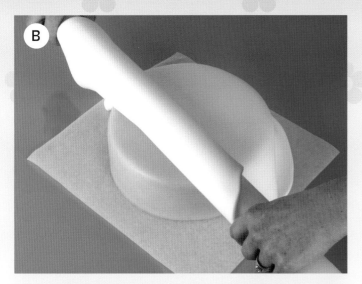

5 Lift and drape the paste over the cake using a rolling pin (**B**). Carefully lift the sides of the paste, brushing the top surface of the cake in one direction to eliminate any air trapped in between. Continue to smooth the top with the palm of your hand and then use a smoother (**C**).

6 For the sides, lift, flatten and rearrange any folds at the bottom removing any creases. Do not smooth downwards as this may cause a tear at the top edge. With your hand, ease the sugarpaste inwards at the base and smooth the sides with an inward motion using your hand and a smoother.

7 Trim the bottom edge with a marzipan knife (**D**). Trim the paste in stages as the icing shrinks back.

8 Check the surface and sides for any flaws and re-smooth if necessary. For air bubbles, insert a pin or fine needle into the bubble at an angle and gently rub the air out, then re-smooth to remove the tiny hole.

9 Once you are happy with the surface, use either the smoother or the palm of your hand and polish the top of the cake to create a glossy finish.

10 Ideally the sugarpaste should be left to dry for one or two days at room temperature before the cake is decorated.

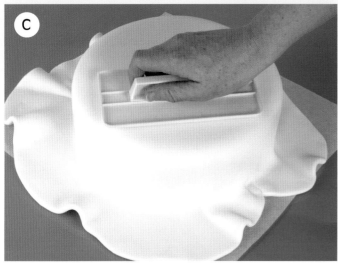

Tip
Keep the dusting of icing (confectioners') sugar on the work surface very light; too much will dry out the paste and make it crack.

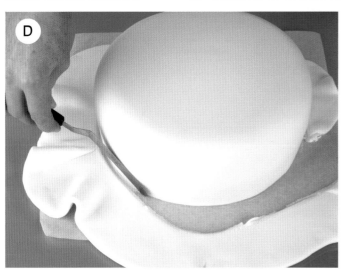

Covering the Cake Board

Moisten the board with cool boiled water, then roll out the specified quantity of sugarpaste to an even thickness, ideally using spacing rods (see page 28). Cover the board completely with sugarpaste using the same method as for the covering of the cake, smoothing the paste out and trimming the edges neatly with a marzipan knife. Some paste can then be saved by removing a circle from the centre of the board, which will be covered by the cake. For a professional finish edge the board with ribbon, securing with non-toxic glue.

Tip

An alternative method for covering a board involves placing the cake on to the board prior to covering them, then using a single piece of sugarpaste to cover them both. The sugarpaste needs to be rolled out much larger for this method.

Covering the cake board in sugarpaste gives your cakes a really professional appearance and allows you to add extra decorations and embellishments. As a finishing touch, edge the board with a length of ribbon.

Covering a Cake with Marzipan

A layer of marzipan is used on fruit cakes only. Sponge cakes should be covered with buttercream (see page 26) prior to covering with sugarpaste. For fruit cakes, coat first with apricot glaze (see page 27) as this will help the marzipan to stick. The quantity of marzipan required will depend on the size of the cake, but as a general guide, half the weight of the cake will give you the correct weight of marzipan.

1 Place the glazed cake on to a sheet of greaseproof paper. Place the marzipan in between spacing rods and roll to an even thickness large enough to cover the cake.

2 Lift the marzipan on to the rolling pin and place it over the cake. Push the marzipan into the sides of the cake using a cupped hand to ensure there are no air pockets.

3 Trim off any excess marzipan with a knife and then run cake smoothers along the sides and the top of the cake until they are straight.

4 Leave the marzipan to dry for one or two days in a cool temperature.

5 Before applying the sugarpaste, sterilize the surface of the cake by brushing the marzipan with a clear spirit such as gin, vodka or kirsch. Ensure the entire surface is moist; if there are any dry areas the paste will not stick to the marzipan and could result in air bubbles.

Tip

If you are using marzipan, make sure nobody eating the cake is allergic to nuts. This is very important as nut allergies are serious and can have fatal consequences.

Dowelling Cakes

A stacked cake is dowelled to avoid the possibility of the upper tiers sinking into the lower tiers. The Cute Christening project (page 69) is the only cake that requires dowelling but you could use this technique to add extra tiers to any of the other cakes, if you want to adapt the designs.

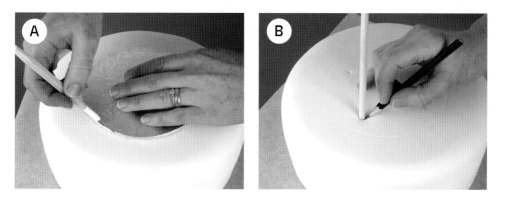

1 Place a cake board the same size as the tier above in the centre of the bottom tier cake. Scribe around the edge of the board (**A**) leaving an outline and then remove the board.

2 Insert a wooden dowel vertically into the cake 2.5cm (1in) from the outline, down to the cake board below. Take a pencil and mark the dowel level with the surface of the cake (**B**) and then remove the dowel.

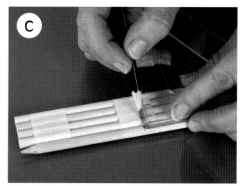

3 Tape together the number of dowels required (four is usually sufficient), and then draw a line across using the marked dowel as a guide (**C**). You can then saw across all the dowels to make them exactly the same length. Alternatively, you can unwrap the marked dowels and cut each of them separately with a pair of pliers or strong kitchen scissors.

4 Place the cut dowel back into the hole, then arrange the other dowels into the three, six and nine o'clock positions to the first one (**D**). Ensure that all the inserted dowels are level and have flat tops.

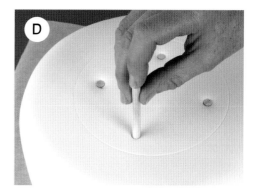

5 The cake board of the upper tier should rest on the dowels and not on the cake. The very slight gap in between the cake and the board of the upper tier will not be noticed and is normally covered by decoration.

Have Your Cake and Eat It!

You may well have cooked up a storm and made the perfect party cake, but how do you get your creation from kitchen to guest without a hitch? Storing the cake ahead of the event is the first consideration, then, if the party is not at your home, transporting it to the venue in one piece is of primary importance. Finally, some top tips follow on cutting the cake and removing items before eating it.

Cake Boxes

The most essential item for safe storage and transportation of your cake is a strong box designed for the job. You can buy special boxes for stacked cakes (see Suppliers, page 126) that open up at the front to enable the cake to slide inside. The front then closes and finally the lid is placed on the top. Make sure the box is deep and high enough to take the cake without damaging it when the lid goes on. To make the cake even safer inside the box, you can buy non-slip matting from most DIY stores. A piece of this cut to size and placed under the cake board will prevent it moving around inside the box.

Tip

Keep your cakes away from direct sunlight at all times, as bright light will fade the sugarpaste.

Room Temperature

The temperature of the room the cake is stored in is crucial to its condition. If your house or the party venue is very humid it can be disastrous. You would do well to invest in a portable dehumidifier to keep the moisture at bay, especially during wet weather. Never think that your figures will benefit from leaving a heater on in the room; you will find that they become too warm and soft and will flop over.

Transportation

If you are transporting a cake, you need to be sure that the boot (trunk) of the car is high enough when closed, and the cake itself is made secure on a flat surface for the journey. Never put the cake on the back seat of the car, as this is not a level surface and the cake could be ruined when you apply the brakes. Remember too that if the vehicle gets too hot, it will affect the cake. It can melt buttercream and make sugarpaste soft.

Cutting the Cake

Many people have no idea how to begin to cut a cake, particularly a stacked one. If it is not cut properly it could end up in a pile of crumbs. The number of portions you require will have some bearing on the way you cut the cake. A simple way is to mark points on the edge of the cake at the desired intervals. Use a sharp serrated knife to cut across the cake and then downwards keeping the blade of the knife clean at all times. Then cut the section into smaller pieces.

The Decorations

If you wish to keep the decorations or figures on the cake, remove them before cutting. If they are to be stored, then do not put them into a plastic container, as they will sweat. Place them inside a clean cardboard box wrapped in tissue paper. Your decorations and figures will keep for a long time if you make sure they are kept in a dry atmosphere. Should you wish to display them, the best place is inside a glass-fronted cabinet where they will be safe.

Any decorations with wires attached should never be inserted directly into the cake as the metal can cause contamination. Instead, insert a cake pick, pushing it right into the cake until the top is level with the surface, then place the wires inside. Alternatively, you can make a mound of sugarpaste to insert wires into, and this can be hidden with more decoration.

When making figures for your cake, never insert cocktail sticks, always use pieces of dry raw spaghetti. Remove these before eating the figures. Children will always want to eat the figures, no matter how long it has taken you to make them.

Tip

If you wish to add candles to decorate your cake, always insert the candle holder into the cake first. When the candles are lit, they will prevent any wax from spilling on to the cake. Remove them before cutting the cake.

Frequently Asked Questions

Q: What if the road I am taking to deliver the cake is very bumpy?
A: Place the cake on a flat surface in the car. If necessary place a foam mat under the box and drive slowly!

Q: Is the footwell of the car the best place to transport a cake?
A: It is a good place, but make sure that there is nothing on the seat to slide off on to the cake – with disastrous consequences.

Q: What if it is a really hot day when the cake is delivered?
A: Keep the air conditioning on if you have it.

Q: If the cake is too heavy for me to lift at my destination what should I do?
A: Never try to lift a large cake on your own; ask if there is a truck available, or even a small table on wheels to place it on.

Q: Where is the cake best displayed?
A: Try to display the cake in a tidy, uncluttered area that will not detract from the cake.

Q: What should I look for once the cake has been assembled?
A: Check that the ribbon around the board is still lined up correctly and has not become loose or dislodged. Make sure your cake topper is securely fixed and perfectly upright.

Q: What shall I do if I make a mark on the cake while I am transporting it to its destination?
A: Always carry a fixing kit with you, which should include edible glue, a little royal icing in a bag, and a few spare decorations you can apply to cover the mark, depending on the design of the cake.

Rocking Dragons

There's nothing like a bit of rock and roll to get a party started. These funky fantasy dragons on rhythm and sax are upping the tempo to get everyone in the dancing mood at a teenage boy's birthday party. Bright colours and crazy characters combine to make a stunning cake that's sure to be snapped up in no time.

"When I play my saxaphone, I soon run out of puff!"

Sugarpaste

★ 1kg 200g (2lb 10¼oz) yellow
★ 300g (10½oz) orange
★ 270g (9½oz) red
★ 120g (4¼oz) blue
★ 65g (2¼oz) mid-brown
★ 50g (1¾oz) black
★ 5g (¼oz) white

Materials

★ 25 x 20cm (10 x 8in) oval cake
★ Edible glue (see page 26)
★ Non-toxic glue

Equipment

★ 30 x 25cm (12 x 10in) oval cake drum
★ 7cm (2¾in) cake cards
★ 2.5cm (1in) and 1.5cm (½in) square cutters
★ 1.5cm (½in) and 1cm (⅜in) round cutters
★ Spool of gold florists' wire
★ Orange ribbon 15mm (½in) wide x 1m (40in) long
★ Basic tool kit (see pages 12–13)

Covering the board and cake...............

1 To cover the board take 125g (4½oz) of yellow sugarpaste and 125g (4½oz) of orange sugarpaste. Break off some small pieces from each colour and place on the work surface. Gently push the colours together to marble them, then roll the mixture out to an even 3mm (⅛in) thickness into a strip measuring 82 x 5cm (32¼ x 2in). Cut a straight edge on either side of the strip and at each end.

2 Moisten the edges of the board with cool boiled water. Attach the strip keeping the straight edge following the line of the board. Finish at the back of the board and overlap the ends. Using tool no.4, cut into both thickness then take off the excess to make a perfect join. Trim the board with a marzipan knife. Set aside to dry.

3 To cover the cake, first prepare the cake then roll out 1kg (2lb 3¼oz) of yellow sugarpaste to an even 5mm (⅛in) thickness. Cover in the usual way (see page 28), using two cake smoothers to achieve a good finish.

4 Attach the cake centrally and firmly on top of the board with strong edible glue. Edge the board with the ribbon, securing it with non-toxic glue.

The border and musical notes . . . .

1 **To make the blue border around the cake** roll out 80g (2⅞oz) of blue sugarpaste to a 5mm (⅛in) thickness. Using a 2.5cm (1in) square cutter, press out some squares. Cut each square in half diagonally to make a triangle shape (**A**). Attach with edible glue around the base of the cake. Set the cake aside to dry.

2 **For the musical notes** you will need two round cutters measuring 1.5cm (½in) and 1cm (⅜in), 26g (1oz) black sugarpaste and 13g (½oz) each of blue, red and orange sugarpaste. Roll out the sugarpaste quite thinly and cut a strip 0.5cm (⅛in) wide. Cut out the two sizes of circles. Make the notes by using a short strip and adding a circle on the end (**B**). Vary the notes in different colours and attach with edible glue around the cake.

3 **To make the treble clef** roll a thin lace of black paste. Place one end down on to the work surface and begin to make the shape using **B** as a guide. Add a small circle at the end to finish and glue to the side of the cake.

4 **Make three smaller notes** to go inside the saxophone and set aside to dry. Take a length of gold florist's wire and twist it around your paintbrush to make a coil, leaving the wire straight at both ends (**B**). Glue the note to one end of the wire and use a small ball of paste to hold it in place. Make three notes on wires and set them aside.

Tip

Vary the colour of the sugarpaste as you make the musical notes to add interest and bring the music to life.

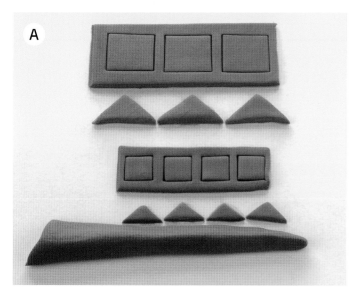

A

B

The saxophone

To make the saxophone you will need 14g (½oz) of mid-brown sugarpaste. Roll into a ball and then into a sausage shape. Narrow two-thirds of the sausage shape leaving one end nice and fat. Make the curved shape of the instrument and push tool no.3 into the end to widen it. Push a short piece of dry spaghetti into the top and add a small black cone for the mouthpiece. Make the keys by adding three small brown strips with two small round balls on either end (**C**). Attach these at intervals down the saxophone. Set aside to dry.

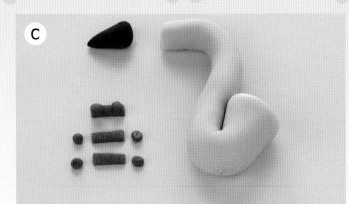

The guitar

1 Make this in advance and allow to dry. Take 50g (1¾oz) of mid-brown sugarpaste and roll out to a 5mm (⅛in) thickness. Cut out a figure-of-eight shape with the top slightly smaller than the bottom (**D**). The final length should be 7cm (2¾in).

2 Roll out 20g (¾oz) of black sugarpaste to measure 0.5 x 9cm (⅛ x 3½in). Set aside to dry then glue the piece to the guitar. Roll some thin strings from the mid-brown paste and glue on the top. Cut a small flat strip to go across the strings near the top (**D**).

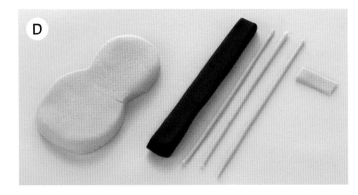

The red dragon

1 For the body roll 120g (4¼oz) of red sugarpaste into a ball and then into a long cone shape. Keep the base fat and do not taper the upper part too much – it should look like a light bulb (**E**). Place the cone on a cake card. Push a piece of dry spaghetti through the body, leaving 2cm (¾in) showing at the top.

2 Make the legs by equally dividing 30g (1oz) of red sugarpaste. Roll into fat cone shapes and bend at the ankles. Flatten the feet slightly, and then using tool no.4, make a 'V' shape in the centre and a diagonal cut on the inside of the outer toes (**E**). Gently roll each toe to soften the edges.

3 For the claws roll three small cone shapes using yellow sugarpaste and attach to the end of each toe (**E**). Push a short piece of dry spaghetti into the hip on either side of the body, add some edible glue and attach the legs, turning the feet out to give some movement.

4 For the tail roll 30g (1oz) of red sugarpaste into a tapered sausage shape, measuring 12.5cm (5in). Pinch a ridge along the top of the tail with your fingers, making a diagonal cut at the thickest end (**A**).

5 Using 20g (¾oz) of blue sugarpaste, cut out some squares with the 1.5cm (½in) square cutter and then cut them in half diagonally (**A**). Attach the triangle shapes along the ridge of the tail securing with edible glue.

6 Push a piece of dry spaghetti into the base of the dragon's body at the back and slip the tail over. Set any leftover blue sugarpaste aside to make the spots.

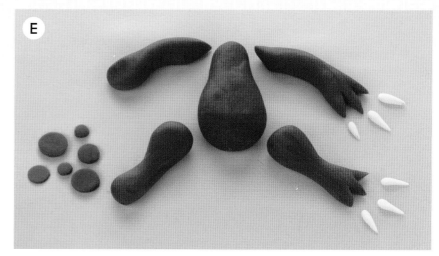

E

Tip

Arrange the tail into a curved shape to give it movement and added style.

7 Make the belly of the dragon using 30g (1oz) of yellow sugarpaste rolled into a long fat cone shape. Flatten slightly with your hand. Using tool no.4, mark lines horizontally across (**F**). Apply some edible glue to the front of the dragon and attach the belly in the centre. Make some blue spots using the two small round cutters and glue all over the body and tail.

8 Take the guitar and place it across the body of the dragon. Push a piece of dry spaghetti into the body to support the guitar and secure with edible glue.

9 For the arms roll 25g (⅞oz) of red sugarpaste into a sausage shape. Make a diagonal cut in the centre and flatten the rounded ends slightly with your finger. Cut out the shape as described for the feet (see page 39) and roll the edges until rounded, then add the claws in yellow (**E**).

10 Push a short piece of dry spaghetti into the top of the body and attach the arms securely over the top. Arrange the hands on the guitar in the correct position and secure with edible glue. You may need some foam to support the guitar until dry.

Tip

If you are short of time, you could choose to make just one of the dragons to attach to a smaller cake for a quirky gift.

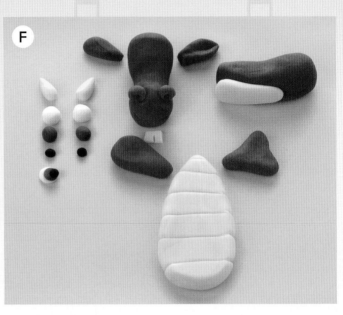

F

The baby dragon

1 For the body roll 70g (2½oz) of orange sugarpaste into a fat cone shape. Place the cone on a cake card. Push a piece of dry spaghetti down through the centre, leaving 2cm (¾in) showing at the top.

2 For the belly roll 30g (1oz) of yellow sugarpaste into a cone shape and flatten with your rolling pin. Using tool no.4, mark the lines across horizontally. Attach to the front of the body with edible glue (**G**).

3 For the legs equally divide 20g (¾oz) of orange sugarpaste and roll each portion into a fat sausage shape. Narrow around the ankle area forming a rounded foot. Press and lift the foot to shape. Push a short piece of dry spaghetti into the hip area of the body and attach the legs with edible glue. Using yellow sugarpaste, add two small round pads to each foot and add the nails (**G**). The baby dragon's foot has no claws just pads and nails.

4 To make the head roll 20g (¾oz) of orange sugarpaste into an oval shape. Narrow the shape in the centre and flatten the front of the snout with your finger (**H**). Push the end of your paintbrush into the centre front of the snout to form a round mouth. Take a very small cone of red sugarpaste and push this into the hole, again pushing the end of your paintbrush into the red paste.

5 For the nostrils add two small balls of orange sugarpaste to the top of the snout and push the end of your paintbrush into them (**H**).

6 For the ears push a short piece of dry spaghetti into either side of the head and make two small cone shapes in orange sugarpaste, pinch them at the top (**H**) and slip the over the spaghetti, securing with edible glue.

7 For the horns and hair add two small yellow sugarpaste cones to the top of the head. Make three cones of orange sugarpaste and place these in between the horns (**H**).

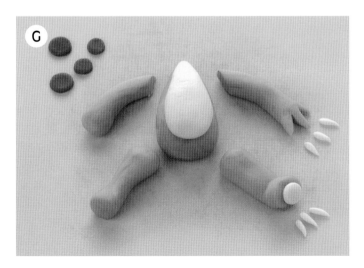

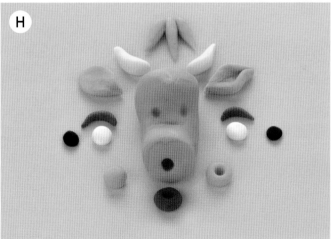

8 For the eyes roll two small white balls, place on the face and add two smaller black balls for the pupils. Add two small banana shapes in red to form the eyelids (**H**). Place the saxophone in front of the dragon and insert the mouthpiece into the mouth.

9 For the arms equally divide 30g (1oz) of orange sugarpaste and roll each piece into a fat sausage shape, pressing the end lightly with your finger. Make the claws as you did for the red dragon (see page 39) (**G**). Apply some edible glue to the inside of the claws and place them on to the saxophone. Drop a small ball of soft sugarpaste into the saxophone and push the musical notes on the gold wires into this.

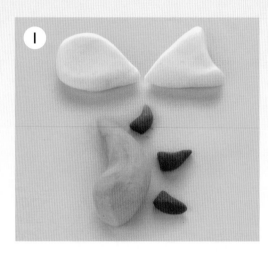

10 Make a short fat tail by rolling 10g (⅜oz) of orange sugarpaste into a curved cone shape. Make a diagonal cut at the fattest end. Push a short piece of dry spaghetti into the back of the dragon and attach the tail with edible glue. Add some little curved red cone shapes to the tail (**I**).

11 For the wings you will need 8g (¼oz) of yellow sugarpaste equally divided. Make each piece into a cone, flatten with your finger and indent to form a wing shape (**I**). Attach the wings to the back of the body with edible glue.

12 Add some red spots all over the dragon using a small round cutter. When dry, gently lift the dragon on to the top of the cake, securing with edible glue.

A Little More Fun!

Dinky Dragons

These fun mini cakes reflect the colour and theme of the large cake. They would make a lovely gift for your guests to take home. They can be baked in the Silverwood multi-mini cake pans (see Suppliers, page 126) or simply be made from slices of a large cake and then served on their own little cake boards. Decorate them in the same way as the main cake, with musical notes, a dragon's head or even a dragon's claw to get the boys roaring for more!

Down on the Farm

It's a beautiful summer's day down on the farm. The pigs,

ducks and sheep are tucking into their tea party, while

the cows are dancing to the sound of their own bells.

This comical cake is perfect for a child's birthday party,

or for any occasion where animal lovers will be present.

"Time for a tea break – that pig sure makes a lovely cuppa!"

You will need

Sugarpaste

* 1kg 750g (3lb 13¾oz) white
* 225g (8oz) light brown
* 220g (7¾oz) dark green
* 120g (4¼oz) peach
* 50g (1¾oz) blue
* 35g (1¼oz) black
* 28g (1oz) dark brown
* 16g (½oz) yellow
* 5g (¼oz) red
* 2g (⅛oz) orange

Materials

* 25 x 10cm (10 x 4in) round cake
* 5cm (2in) square mini cake
* Green paste food colour
* Black liquid food colour
* Pink dust food colour
* 12g (½oz) sugar flower paste (see page 25)
* White vegetable fat (shortening)
* Confectioners' glaze
* Edible glue (see page 26)
* Non-toxic glue

Equipment

* 36cm (14in) round cake drum
* Sugar press (or garlic press)
* Cutting wheel (or pizza cutter)
* Floppy mat (or freezer bag)
* Cel pad and cel stick
* Daisy-textured rolling pin
* 4cm (1½in), 3cm (1¼in), 2.5cm (1in), 2cm (¾in), 1.5cm (½in) and 1cm (⅜in) round cutters
* 2.5cm (1in) daisy cutter
* 2.5cm (1in) square cutter (optional)
* Green spotted ribbon 15mm (½in) wide x 115cm (45in) long
* Basic tool kit (see pages 12–13)

Covering the boards and cake.........

1 To cover the cake take 1kg 500g (3lb 5oz) of white sugarpaste and colour it with a bright green paste food colour, knead together until the paste colour is evenly dispersed. Take off 1kg 200g (2lb 10¼oz) and roll out. The remainder will cover the board. Cover the cake in the usual way (see page 28), trimming the edges neatly.

2 To make the border around the side of the cake you will need 220g (7¾oz) of dark green sugarpaste. Roll out into two lengths measuring 43 x 6cm (17 x 2⅜in) and make a straight edge for the base of the border.

3 Using a cutting wheel (or a pizza cutter), begin to shape the top of the border in a wavy and irregular line (**A**). Shape the second border in the same way, making sure the beginning and end of the borders are the same height so that they will join neatly. Apply some edible glue to the back of each piece and attach to the cake, keeping the joins on either side of the cake. Place the cake on to a sheet of greaseproof paper to dry.

4 To cover the board use the remaining bright green sugarpaste and roll out into a strip measuring 105 x 6cm (41 x 2⅜in). Apply some cool boiled water to the edge of the board and then lay the strip around, easing in the folds towards the centre and making them smooth. Make a neat join at the back of the board and then trim the edges with your knife, setting any off-cuts aside for use later.

5 Attach the cake to the centre of the board with strong edible glue (see tip page 26). Edge the board with the ribbon, securing it with non-toxic glue.

The daisies and clouds

1 Make nine daisies using a 2.5cm (1in) daisy cutter and 12g (½oz) of sugar flower paste. Roll the paste out thinly and dust with icing (confectioners') sugar. Press the cutter into the paste and, keeping the pressure on the cutter, move it backwards and forwards on the work surface to make sure you have made a clean cut, and then remove the flower and place it under a floppy mat (or a freezer bag) to prevent it drying out.

2 Place the flower on top of a cel pad (or firm foam), and using a cel stick (or a cocktail stick), roll each petal sideways to thin out and widen. Place the flower into a paint tray to shape it and leave until dry. Roll nine small balls of yellow sugarpaste to make the centres of the flowers, securing with edible glue (**A**). Set aside to dry.

3 For the clouds roll out 15g (½oz) of white sugarpaste and cut out some random fluffy cloud shapes. Soften the edges with your finger and attach them to the sides of the cake with edible glue.

The fence

1 To complete the fence you will need 20g (¾oz) of blue sugarpaste rolled out into a rectangle shape. Cut out three strips measuring 1 x 6cm (⅜ x 2⅜in). Cut off 1cm (⅜in) at the top. Using tool no.4, mark each strip to look like wood using downward strokes, and then make two diagonal cuts at the top. Attach the three posts to the side of the cake with edible glue, leaving a gap of 1cm (⅜in) to insert two of the short pieces in between the posts (**B**).

2 Attach three daisies beside the fence and four on the other side of the cake. Set one daisy aside for the cows to hold.

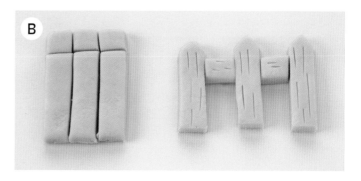

The small cow

1 To complete the cow you will need 5g (¼oz) of white sugarpaste, 1g (⅛oz) of peach, 1g (⅛oz) of light brown and 1g (⅛oz) of black. Take off 3g (⅛oz) of white sugarpaste and roll into a ball for the head. Roll a small oval shape from the peach sugarpaste and attach to the front of the head securing with edible glue, pushing the end of your paintbrush into the corners to make the nostrils (**C**).

2 For the bottom lip roll another small peach oval shape and place underneath (**C**). Push a short piece of dry spaghetti into the side of the cake above the fence, where the head is to be placed. Apply some edible glue and slip the head over the spaghetti.

3 For the ears divide 1g (⅛oz) of white sugarpaste equally and roll two small cone shapes. Place on either side of the head, then press the end of your paintbrush inside each ear to mark and secure (**C**).

4 For the eyes roll two small balls of white sugarpaste and place them above the nose. Add two small black pupils (**C**).

5 For the horns and hair make two small cone shapes using 1g (⅛oz) of light brown sugarpaste equally divided, attaching them just above the ears (**C**). Add three thin black cone shapes on top of the head.

6 For the tail roll 1g (⅛oz) of white sugarpaste into a tapered cone shape. Make a diagonal cut at one end and attach to the fence. Add a small cone shape of black sugarpaste at the end of the tail, marking the hairs with tool no.4 (**C**).

The dancing cows

1 To complete two cows you will need 100g (3½oz) of white sugarpaste, 20g (¾oz) of peach, 10g (⅜oz) of black and 2g (⅛oz) of light brown. To make the body of the cow with one leg, take off 20g (¾oz) of white sugarpaste and roll into a cone shape. Pull out the leg at the widest end of the cone with your finger and thumb to form a sausage shape. When the leg is long enough, bend to shape the knee, and make a straight cut at the end (**C**). Push a short piece of dry spaghetti into the end of the leg.

2 For the hoof take off 1g (⅛oz) of peach sugarpaste and roll into a cone shape. Make a straight cut at the widest end of the cone and attach with edible glue over the spaghetti. Using tool no.4, split the hoof at the front (**C**).

3 Push a piece of dry spaghetti into the side of the cake where the first cow is to be positioned. Apply some edible glue to the back of the body and slip it over the spaghetti, making sure that the hoof is resting on the cake board.

4 Make the other back leg using 8g (¼oz) of white sugarpaste rolled into a long cone shape, bending it slightly at the knee (**C**). Push a piece of dry spaghetti into the top of the body where you are going to attach the leg, bringing it across the front of the body, and then push a short piece of dry spaghetti into the end of the leg. Add another hoof using 1g (⅛oz) of peach sugarpaste and support with some foam until dry.

5 Make a small udder using 2g (⅛oz) of peach sugarpaste rolled into a ball. Push a short piece of dry spaghetti into the base of the cow and attach the udder. Add three tiny balls of peach sugarpaste for the teats (**C**).

6 Make the tail in the same way as for the small cow (see page 48).

7 Make the front legs using 10g (⅜oz) of white sugarpaste rolled into a sausage shape. Make a diagonal cut in the centre and a straight cut at each end (**C**). Bend the outside leg at the knee area and bring it forwards to rest on the leg at the front of the body. The other leg, which is

on the inside, is also bent at the knee area and shaped a little more to give it movement.

8 Attach a small hoof at the end of each leg using 2g (⅛oz) of peach sugarpaste equally divided as before, and then secure into place with edible glue (**C**).

9 Make the head in the same way as the small cow's head (**C**), but using 6g (¼oz) of white sugarpaste for the head and 4g (⅛oz) of peach for the nose.

10 Using a no.00 paintbrush and some black liquid food colour, outline the eyes of the cow, adding the eyelashes. Dip a soft clean brush into some pink dust food colour, dust inside the nostrils and ears, and blush the cheeks.

11 For the cow patches use 4g (⅛oz) of black sugarpaste. Take off small amounts to make irregular shapes and glue to the body randomly.

12 Make a second cow with a reversed body so that they are dancing with each other. Attach a daisy in between their hands.

The cowbells

1 To make two cowbells you will need 4g (⅛oz) of blue and 2g (⅛oz) of yellow sugarpaste. Roll out and cut a narrow strip of blue sugarpaste measuring 5cm (2in) long to make the ribbon. Fold the strip into a 'V' shape (**D**) and attach the ends over the shoulders of the cow, bringing it over to the left or right side of the cow to give it movement.

2 To make the bell roll a small ball of yellow sugarpaste. Take tool no.3 and push the pointed end into the ball to hollow it out (**D**). Attach the bell to the end of the ribbon. Make two.

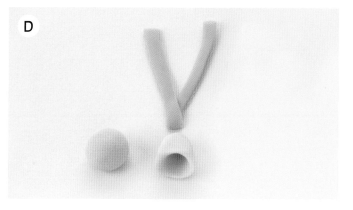

D

The mini cake bale of hay

1 Cover the mini cake using 80g (2⅞oz) of light brown sugarpaste. To make the straw covering you will need a further 125g (4½oz) of light brown sugarpaste and a sugar press (or garlic press).

2 Cover the top and two long sides by extruding strands the width of the bale, and then attach them horizontally over the surface. Decorate the ends of the bale by extruding very short lengths of paste from the press. Using tool no.4, chop the strands off with a downward movement and apply them to the ends of the bale (**E**).

3 Make the tablecloth by rolling out 35g (1¼oz) of white sugarpaste. Run a daisy-textured rolling pin over the surface, and then cut out a square measuring 3.5cm (1⅜in), and run a stitch wheel around the edges, or use tool no.12 (**E**). Place the cloth on the top of the bale and set the off-cuts aside for use later.

The sandwich

Roll out 8g (¼oz) of light brown sugarpaste and cut out two squares measuring 2.5cm (1in). Take a pinch of green (leftover from covering the board) and red sugarpaste and place on the top of one square to look like lettuce and tomato. Place the second square on the top and then cut in half diagonally. Using tool no.11, take out a bite from one half of the sandwich and set aside. Cut the remaining half into two again (**E**) and set aside until required.

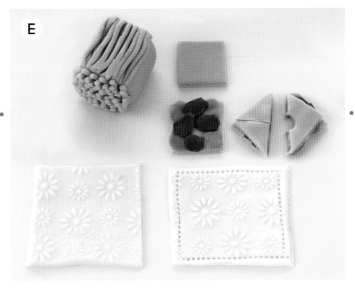

E

The tableware

1 To complete all the items you will need 24g (⅞oz) of blue sugarpaste. To make the teapot, take off 5g (¼oz) and roll into a ball. Roll a small sausage for the spout and curve it. Attach to the body of the teapot. Roll another small sausage and curve for the handle, attach on the opposite side. Roll out the remainder and then cut out the lid using a 1.5cm (½in) round cutter. Add a small knob to the top and attach to the top of the teapot (**F**). Set aside to dry.

2 To make three cups take off 3g (⅛oz) of blue sugarpaste and roll equally into three balls. Using tool no.3, insert the pointed end into each ball to hollow it out. Make three small sausage shapes and join the ends together for the cup handles, then attach to the cups (**F**).

3 To make one large plate roll out the remainder of the blue sugarpaste and cut out a 4cm (1½in) circle. Lightly press a 3cm (1¼in) round cutter into the centre of the plate to mark the rim (**F**). Use this plate for the chocolate cake.

4 Cut out another plate using a 3cm (1¼in) round cutter, press a 2.5cm (1in) round cutter into the centre to mark the rim. Use this plate for the jam tarts.

5 Cut out a further four 2cm (¾in) circles for the tea plates, and three 1.5cm (½in) circles for the saucers. Place the ball end of tool no.3 into the centre of each saucer using a circular movement to make a small hollow (**F**).

6 Stack three tea plates and two saucers on top of each other, and then attach two stacked cups on the top and set aside. Put the sandwich on to the final tea plate and save one cup and saucer until required.

The chocolate cake

1 Roll out 28g (1oz) of dark brown sugarpaste to a 5mm thickness, and cut out two circles, using a 3cm (1¼in) round cutter (**F**). Save the off-cuts for use later.

2 Cut out another 3cm (1¼in) circle using 1g (⅛oz) of red sugarpaste, and another using 1g (⅛oz) of white sugarpaste. Sandwich the red and white circles in between the dark brown circles to form the cake.

3 Decorate the top of the cake with 1g (⅛oz) of white sugarpaste rolled into small balls and arranged evenly, then add smaller balls of red on top for the cherries (**F**).

The jam tarts

1 To make seven tarts you will need 6g (¼oz) of light brown sugarpaste and 1g (⅛oz) of red. Roll out the light brown sugarpaste and then cut out seven circles using a 1cm (⅜in) round cutter. Hollow out the centre of each circle using the ball end of tool no.3. Add a small ball of red in the centre of each and flatten slightly with your finger (**F**).

2 Paint the tops of the tarts and the cherries on the cake with confectioners' glaze. To give a deep shine, add one coat, let it dry and then add a second coat.

Setting the table

1 Attach the chocolate cake on its plate to one corner of the table and the stacked tableware on the opposite site.

2 Place the teapot in front of the cake to the right side where the pig will be able to reach it.

3 Secure the plate of jam tarts in front of the stacked tableware with edible glue.

4 Push two pieces of dry spaghetti down into the centre of the cake and position the hay bale on top, securing with edible glue.

The lying pig

1 To complete the pig you will need 48g (1⅝oz) of peach sugarpaste. Take off 16g (½oz) and roll into a cone shape for the body (**G**). Place this down on to the work surface. Push a short piece of dry spaghetti into the top of the cone to support the head.

2 For the back legs equally divide 8g (¼oz) of peach sugarpaste and roll into two fat cone shapes. Narrow the lower half of each cone to shape the leg, and make a straight cut at the end. Push a short piece of dry spaghetti into the end of each leg. Bend the legs half way down into a bent position, and then attach to the back of the pig (**G**).

3 For the front legs roll 6g (¼oz) of peach sugarpaste into a sausage shape and make a diagonal cut in the centre. Push a short piece of dry spaghetti into each end and attach to the front of the pig (**G**).

4 For the hooves add a pinch of red sugarpaste to 3g (⅛oz) of peach to make a deeper shade. Roll four small cone shapes. Apply some edible glue to the end of the legs and attach the hooves. Using tool no.4, split the front of each hoof (**G**).

5 For the tail roll a small ball of peach sugarpaste into a thin lace, and then curl it around the end of your paintbrush. Slip it off and attach with edible glue to the back of the pig (**G**).

G

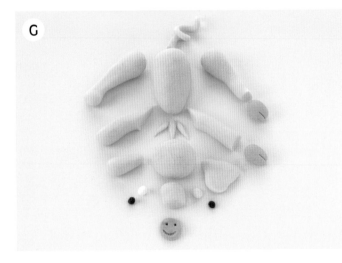

6 For the head take off 12g (½oz) of peach sugarpaste and roll into a smooth ball (**G**). Slip over the spaghetti at the neck. Push a short piece of dry spaghetti into the centre of the head.

7 For the snout take off 1g (⅛oz) of peach sugarpaste and roll into a short sausage shape, and then flatten both ends. Slip the snout over the spaghetti and secure with edible glue. Roll a small ball of the deeper pink sugarpaste and flatten with your finger. Glue this to the front of the snout. Mark two nostrils with tool no.5 and then add a small mouth underneath using tool no.11 (**G**).

8 For the eyes add two small balls of white sugarpaste and place above and on either side of the snout. Add small dark brown pupils on top so the pig looks cross-eyed (**G**).

9 For the ears equally divide 2g (⅛oz) of peach sugarpaste and roll into two cone shapes. Flatten the shapes with your fingers and shape into a curve at the widest end (**G**). Attach to each side of the head, bringing the ears forwards.

10 For the hair roll three thin cone shapes and attach in between the ears (**G**). Secure the completed pig with edible glue along the side of the hay bale.

The standing pig

1 The proportions are just the same as for the lying pig, but to complete this pig you will need to add some-extra CMC (Tylose) to the paste to strengthen it (see page 9).

2 For the body make the cone shape and then push a length of dry spaghetti through the body leaving 2cm (¾in) showing at the top. Also push a short piece into the hip and set aside.

3 Shape the two back legs as before, but keeping them straighter. Push a piece of dry spaghetti down through the centre of each leg, leaving a little showing at the end of the leg but not at the top. Add the hooves over the spaghetti at the end of the legs. Attach the legs securely at the hip and rest the body on a piece of foam to support it so that the shape does not flatten while you are working on the other parts.

4 Roll the arms and attach the hooves as before. Stand the body on top of the lying pig and mark where the hooves will rest. Push a short piece of dry spaghetti into the back of the lying pig where you have marked the holes. Apply some edible glue around these spots and carefully push the pig's hooves over the top of the spaghetti. Place a piece of foam in between the front of the pig and the hay bale, so that the standing pig will stay upright until dry.

5 Attach the right arm to the pig and place the hoof on to the teapot to help support the pig. Attach the left arm and place the hoof so that it is holding the plate of tarts.

6 Complete the head as described for the lying pig and slip over the spaghetti at the neck being careful not to disturb the rest of the body.

The sheep

1 To complete the sheep you will need 63g (2¼oz) of white sugarpaste and 24g (⅞oz) of black. Take off 28g (1oz) of white sugarpaste and roll into a cone shape for the body (**H**). Place the body against the side of the hay bale and secure with edible glue. Push a piece of dry spaghetti down through the centre, leaving 2cm (¾in) showing at the top. Apply edible glue to the front and side of the body.

2 For the wool soften 35g (1¼oz) of white sugarpaste with white vegetable fat (shortening) and fill the cup of the sugar press (or garlic press). Extrude short lengths and chop them off with tool no.4, and attach to the body. Push a short piece of dry spaghetti into the side of the body at the top and bottom to secure the legs.

3 For the legs take off 8g (¼oz) of black sugarpaste and roll into a sausage shape measuring 18cm (7in) long. Cut in half and in half again making four legs (**H**). Push a short piece of dry spaghetti into the end of each leg.

4 To make the hooves equally divide 6g (¼oz) of the black sugarpaste into four and roll into oval shapes (**H**). Slip the hooves over the spaghetti and secure with glue. Set aside one of the completed legs and cover to prevent drying. Attach two legs to the lower body and bend at the knee area. Secure the hooves to the top of the cake. Attach the third leg to the top right of the body bending at the elbow and bring it forward. Open the hoof and glue the blue cup inside resting it on the front of the body. Close the hoof around the handle of the cup.

5 For the head take off 8g (¼oz) of black sugarpaste and roll into a cone shape. Using tool no.4, mark a line in the centre front of the cone, and then make two diagonal lines at the top of the line to form a 'V' shape for the nose. Make two small holes where the eyes are to go, and fill with small balls of leftover white sugarpaste. Add two black pupils on the top (**H**). Place the head over the spaghetti at the neck and position it so that it is looking to the left.

6 For the ears divide 2g (⅛oz) of black sugarpaste equally and roll into ovals. Push a short piece of spaghetti into each side of the head and slip the ears over. Press the end of your paintbrush into each ear to mark and secure it.

H

7 Secure the left arm to the body and bend at the elbow. Open the hoof and insert the sandwich with the bite taken out of it. Push the sandwich towards the sheep's mouth and secure with edible glue. Glue the saucer in front of the sheep and the plate with the other half of sandwich on it to the side of the sheep. Drop a small ball of light brown sugarpaste into the cup and flatten gently with your finger.

The mother duck ·

1 To complete the mother duck you will need 30g (1oz) of white sugarpaste and 1g (⅛oz) of yellow. Take off 20g (¾oz) of white sugarpaste and roll into a fat cone shape for the body. Gently pull out the neck from the fattest end of the cone (**I**). Push a piece of dry spaghetti down through the neck to give it support, leaving 2cm (¾in) showing at the top.

2 To make the two wings take off 4g (⅛oz) of white sugarpaste and divide equally. Roll into two cone shapes, and then flatten with your finger to form a curve. Take tool no.4 and mark the feathers (**I**). Attach the wings to each side of the body keeping them quite flat.

3 For the head use 6g (¼oz) of white sugarpaste and roll into a fat cone shape. Keep the pointed end at the top and then pinch out the cheeks with your fingers (**I**).

4 For the beak use 1g (⅛oz) of yellow sugarpaste, make a cone shape and then flatten with your finger. Shape the top of the beak (**I**). Push a short piece of dry spaghetti into the front of the head and slip the beak over, securing with edible glue. Roll a very small cone shape for the base of the beak and attach underneath.

5 For the eyes make two small holes in the front of the head and fill with small balls of white sugarpaste. Finally add small black pupils (**I**).

6 Outline the eyes and add some eyelashes using a no.00 paintbrush and some black liquid food colour. Attach the completed duck to the top of the cake.

7 Make two small feet using 1g (⅛oz) of orange sugarpaste equally divided. Roll two small cone shapes and flatten with your finger. Using tool no.4, make a 'V' shape in the centre and a diagonal cut on either side to form the webbed feet (**I**). Make a straight cut at the top of each foot and glue underneath the duck.

Tip

If you the pupils are hard to pick up with your fingers, dip a brush into some edible glue and pick up the ball on the end, then place it directly into the hole.

The ducklings

1 To complete the four ducklings you will need 12g (½oz) of yellow sugarpaste and 1g (⅛oz) of orange. Take off 1g (⅛oz) of yellow sugarpaste and roll it into a cone shape for the body making a small neck (**J**). Push a short piece of dry spaghetti into the neck leaving 1cm (⅜in) showing to support the head.

2 For the wings equally divide 1g (⅛oz) and set the remaining 1g (⅛oz) aside for the head. Make two small cone shapes and mark with tool no.4, as described for the mother duck (**J**) (see page 55). Attach to each side of the body.

3 For the head roll the remainder of the yellow sugarpaste into a ball and place over the spaghetti at the neck (**J**).

4 For the beak take a pinch of the orange and roll into a very small cone shape, make a straight cut at the widest end and attach to the front of the head (**J**).

5 For the feet roll two small cone shapes using the orange sugarpaste and mark the feet as described for the mother duck (**J**) (see page 55). Attach underneath the body.

6 For the eyes make two small holes in the front of the head and then roll two small balls in black sugarpaste (**J**) and press them on with your finger.

7 Complete the remaining ducklings in the same way and attach them to the cake. Place one on top of the sheep's head, securing with edible glue.

J

Tip
When marking the wings, make sure you work in a diagonal direction using tool no.4 from the tip towards the thickest end.

A Little More Fun!

Farmyard Friends

The wonderful characters from the main cake can be used to decorate fun mini cakes as well. Cover the cakes with strands of light brown sugarpaste extruded through a sugar press to create little hay bales, or alternatively use green sugarpaste and decorate them with daisies. The kids will adore them!

Butterfly Fairy

Girls of all ages love fairies and this pretty cake will help bring the belief alive at any young girl's birthday celebration. The enchanting fairy sits on top of a rainbow-coloured toadstool house, and has exquisite butterfly wings that sparkle in the light, helping to grant the birthday girl's wish on her special day.

"A magical birthday wish from the enchanting fairy."

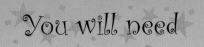

You will need

Sugarpaste

* 1kg 650g (3lb 10¼oz) white
* 340g (12oz) mid-brown
* 155g (5½oz) Lincoln green
* 30g (1oz) blue
* 10g (⅜oz) black
* 5g (¼oz) yellow
* 1g (⅛oz) pink

Materials

* 25cm (10in) hexagonal cake
* Paste food colour in lime green, pink, turquoise, chestnut and white
* Dust food colour in light brown, moss green, pale blue, lime green, purple and pink
* Metallic dust food colour in silver lustre and snowflake
* Clear alcohol
* 60g (2oz) sugar flower paste (see page 25)
* Green Magic Sparkle Flakes
* White vegetable fat (shortening)
* Edible glue (see page 26)
* Non-toxic glue

Equipment

* 32cm (13in) hex cake drum
* 3.5cm (1⅜in) and 1.5cm (½in) butterfly cutters
* 2cm (¾in) and 1.5cm (½in) blossom cutters
* 1cm (⅜in) oval cutter
* 5cm (2in), 4cm (1½in) and 2cm (¾in) round cutters
* Flower stamens: 6 pearl, 2 gold, 1 small white
* Sugar press (or garlic press)
* Green ribbon 15mm (½in) wide x 115cm (45in) long
* Basic tool kit (see pages 12–13)

Covering the board and cake . . . .

1 To cover the board colour 500g (1lb 1½oz) of white sugarpaste with lime green paste food colour and knead well to disperse the colour evenly. Roll out the sugarpaste to an even thickness then cover the board in the usual way (see page 30). Save any leftover sugarpaste to use for decoration. Edge the board with the ribbon, securing it with non-toxic glue.

2 To cover the cake knead together 1kg (2lb 3¼oz) of white sugarpaste with 200g (7oz) of mid-brown to make a deep cream colour. Cover the cake in the usual way (see page 28), using cake smoothers on each section for a good finish. Trim the edge of the cake with a marzipan knife and then transfer the cake to the centre of the board, securing it with strong edible glue (see tip page 26). Set the remaining cream sugarpaste aside for use later.

3 Dust the board and top of the cake lightly with light brown and moss green dust food colour.

Tip

When applying dust food colour to a large area, a fat dusting brush will give the best results.

Decorating the board ·

1 Take a 3.5cm (1⅜in) butterfly cutter and press it into the paste on each corner of the board to outline the shape. Mix together a small amount of silver lustre dust food colour with clear alcohol. Paint over the shape of the butterfly to make a reflection and then leave to dry (**A**). Wash the brush out with clean water.

A

Tip

Before you cut out the six butterflies, make a form to hold the wings in shape. To do this, cut out a length of cardboard measuring 20 x 6cm (8 x 2⅜in). Mark a line down the centre and fold the card lengthways to form a V shape. Support the card with some sugarpaste on either side to keep it level.

2 To make the six butterflies you will need 16g (½oz) of sugar flower paste rolled out very thinly. Cut out the shapes with the 3.5cm (1⅜in) butterfly cutter and place them into a cardboard form (see tip, above right) to support the wings. When dry, paint the upper wing of each butterfly with some pale blue dust food colour mixed with clear alcohol, and the lower wing with lime green dust food colour also mixed with clear alcohol, keeping a separate brush for each colour you are using (**A**).

3 To colour the butterflies take a no.00 paintbrush moistened with clean water, making quite sure there is no excess moisture on the brush. Drag the point of the brush downwards to make a line in the centre of the upper wing, and then make a smaller line on either side. Repeat this on the lower wing. This will remove the colour and form a textured pattern (**A**). Place each butterfly back into the cardboard form each time.

4 To complete the painted decoration you will need some purple dust food colour mixed with clear alcohol, adding some dots to the wings and then painting them carefully using upward strokes with your paintbrush.

5 To complete each butterfly roll a thin cone of black sugarpaste narrowing at the end and secure to the centre with clear alcohol (**A**). Place each butterfly back into the cardboard form to dry.

6 Remove the dried butterflies from the cardboard form and attach over the centre of the butterfly outline on the board, securing with edible glue. Place a short piece of dry spaghetti underneath each wing to give support until set.

Tip

Using dust food colours mixed with clear alcohol allows the paint to dry quickly. This is usually an advantage when you want to get on with the next step. It also gives a more translucent look.

The side decoration

1 To make the foliage roll out 12g (½oz) of the lime green sugarpaste leftover from covering the board into a 5cm (2in) square, then cut out deep 'V' shapes. Divide each shape two or three times to multiply the leaves. Using tool no.4, mark each leaf with a line down the centre (**B**). Make six. Glue the finished pieces to each of the corners of the cake, giving the foliage some movement by bending and curling the pieces.

2 For the grass fill the sugar press (or garlic press) with 10g (⅜oz) of lime green sugarpaste softened with white vegetable fat (shortening). Extrude some short lengths and then cut them off (**B**). Form a line of grass and attach in front of the foliage.

3 Push a short piece of dry spaghetti into the centre of each panel, just 2cm (¾in) from the base of the cake. These will support the caterpillars.

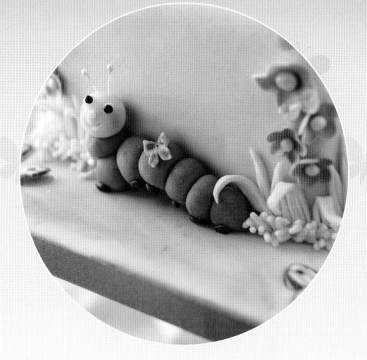

The flowers

1 To make the flowers colour 15g (½oz) of sugar flower paste with pink paste food colour. Cut out six flowers using a 2cm (¾in) blossom cutter and twelve flowers using a 1.5cm (½in) blossom cutter. Cover each blossom with a floppy mat (or a freezer bag) until needed to prevent it drying out.

2 Colour 12g (½oz) of sugar flower paste with blue paste food colour and cut out six flowers with the 2cm (¾in) blossom cutter, and six with the 1.5cm (½in) blossom cutter.

3 Place each flower on top of a cel pad (or a piece of firm foam) and using tool no.1, thin out the edges of each petal with the ball of the tool half on and half off the edge of the flower. Add a small amount of edible glue to the centre of each flower and then place a ball of yellow sugarpaste on top (**B**). Dust the centres with snowflake metallic dust food colour. Attach the flowers as shown down the six corners of the cake using edible glue.

B

The caterpillars . . . .

1 To complete six caterpillars you will need 150g (5¼oz) of Lincoln green sugarpaste, 30g (1oz) of lime green and 5g (¼oz) of black. For each caterpillar take off 25g (⅞oz) of Lincoln green sugarpaste and roll six or seven balls of equal size. Line the balls in an arch shape and place a small cone at the end. Attach together with edible glue (**C**).

2 For the head roll 5g (¼oz) of lime green sugarpaste into a ball and place on the top. Add a small oval-shaped nose and glue to the centre of the head. Using tool no.12, mark a smile. Add two small white balls for the eyes and top with two tiny balls of black for the pupils. Cut a pearl flower stamen in half and push into the top of the head (**C**). Dust the cheeks with pink dust food colour on a dry brush. Make six.

C

Tip

If the paste you have rolled for the head has gone a little too hard to push the stamen into it, take a straight pin and make a small hole; the stamen will then go in very easily.

3 Apply some edible glue to the back of the caterpillar and push the middle of the body over the spaghetti on the side of the cake. Arrange the caterpillar into an arch shape. Using black sugarpaste, roll some tiny oval shapes for the feet and glue one to the underside of each ball. Using a 1.5cm (½in) butterfly cutter and some oddments of colour, cut out a shape and glue to the back of the caterpillar. Add some dots of purple dust food colour mixed with clear alcohol to decorate (**C**).

4 Add a little more grass underneath the arch of the caterpillar to hide the edge of the cake. When you have completed all the side decorations, dust the grass, leaves and the caterpillar lightly using a dry brush and some snowflake metallic dust food colour to give them sparkle.

The mushroom house . . . .

1 To make the mushroom mix together 125g (4½oz) of mid-brown sugarpaste with 60g (2oz) of white to make a light brown shade. Take off 100g (3½oz) and roll into a fat sausage shape to form the stalk (**D**). Push a piece of dry spaghetti down through the centre leaving 2cm (¾in) showing at the top.

2 Roll out 6g (¼oz) of white sugarpaste into a strip long enough to fit around the top of the mushroom stalk. Using a frilling tool or cocktail stick, frill the lower edge (**D**). Trim the depth of the frill to 7mm (¼in). Apply edible glue around the top of the stalk and arrange the frill to meet in a neat join at the back.

3 For the top of the muchroom roll the remaining light brown sugarpaste into a ball and then flatten with the palm of your hand. Keeping the rounded shape, mould the top of the mushroom so that it is domed at the top and soft around the edges. Mark a vertical line at intervals around the edge using tool no.4 (**D**). Dust the top, stalk and underside of the mushroom with patches of pink, lime green and pale blue dust food colour. Apply some edible glue to the top of the stalk, and slip the top of the mushroom over, arching it softly at the front.

4 For the door make a light brown shade by mixing 25g (⅞oz) of white sugarpaste with 14g (½oz) of mid-brown. Take off 5g (¼oz) and set the rest aside. Roll into an oval shape then cut out a shape to measure 5 x 2.5cm (2 x 1in) to make the door. Cut a straight edge down each side and at the bottom, leaving the rounded shape at the top (**D**).

5 To decorate the door apply a coat of edible glue to the front. Cut some narrow strips of pink, blue, green, yellow and white sugarpaste and lay them side-by-side on top of the door, in no particular order, keeping the rounded shape at the top. Trim the door to a length of 3.5cm (1⅜in) and keep the off-cuts to make the windowsills. Add two hinges in pink to the top and bottom of the door, and then add a small knob on the opposite side (**D**). Attach the door to the centre of the mushroom stalk.

6 For the windows roll out 5g (¼oz) of blue sugarpaste and cut out two more small arched shapes. Using tool no.4, make a crisscross pattern over the surface (**D**). Attach a window on either side of the mushroom stalk. Secure the windowsills underneath each window to finish.

D

The stepping stones and small caterpillar . . . .

1 For the stepping stones randomly mix together 24g (⅞oz) of the remaining light brown sugarpaste with a pinch of the blue, pink, yellow and green sugarpaste to make the stones around the mushroom. Take off 8g (¼oz) and make an oval-shaped stone for the small caterpillar to sit on. Place this to the right side of the cake then add flat stones decreasing in size leading from the front door to make a pathway. Add some clumps of grass around the stones and the base of the mushroom. Using the small blossom cutter, add a few flowers alongside the grass (**E**).

2 To make the small caterpillar sitting on the stone you will need 3g (⅛oz) of Lincoln green sugarpaste and 1g (⅛oz) of lime green. Roll four or five balls and a small cone for the tail, and arrange them as before. Add a ball of lime green sugarpaste for the head. Complete the head with the white flower stamens as before (**E**) (see page 64). Attach the small caterpillar to the top of the stone with edible glue.

Fairy Wing Template

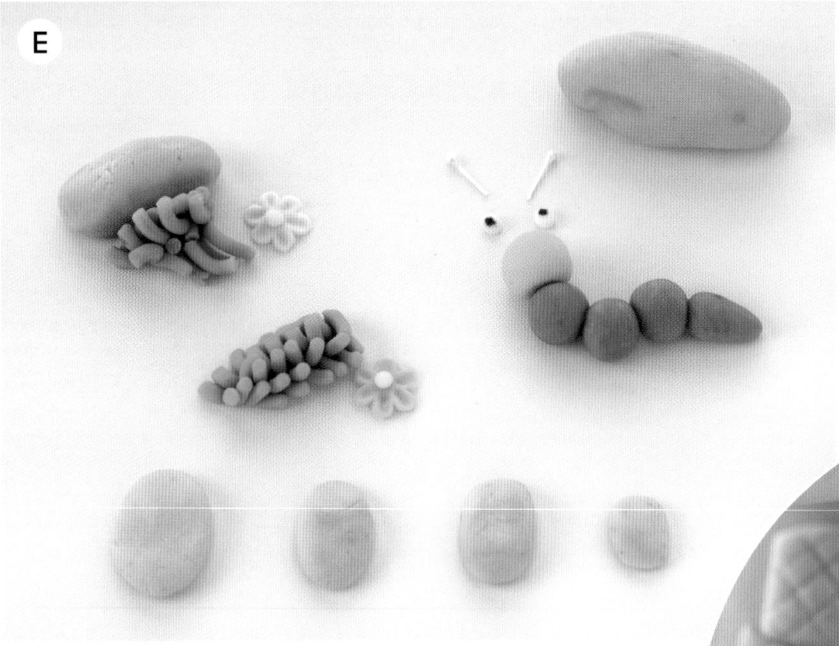

E

The butterfly fairy wings

1 To complete the wings you will need 16g (½oz) of sugar flower paste rolled out thinly. Trace the template opposite, place it on top of the paste, and using a cutting wheel (or pizza cutter), follow the outline of the template. Cut two. Using a 1cm (⅜in) oval cutter, press lightly into the wings forming a row of shapes down the edge (**F**). Place the wings on a flat surface and allow to dry.

2 To decorate the wings dust their surfaces with lime green dust food colour using a soft brush. Take another brush and dust inside the oval shapes with a pink dust food colour. Mix together some moss green dust food colour with clear alcohol, and using a no.4 paintbrush, paint all around the edges of the wings, bringing the brushstrokes from the edge inwards (**F**). Set aside to dry.

3 Enhance the surface of the wings with some Magic Sparkle Flakes. To do this, add a small amount of edible glue to your paintbrush, being careful not to make it too wet otherwise it will dissolve the flakes. Place dots of glue where you are going to apply the flakes. Sprinkle some flakes on to a clean sheet of paper and scatter over the wings allowing the flakes to make contact with the moistened surface. Use enough flakes to make the wings glitter (**F**). Set the wings aside on a flat surface to dry out completely until they are quite hard.

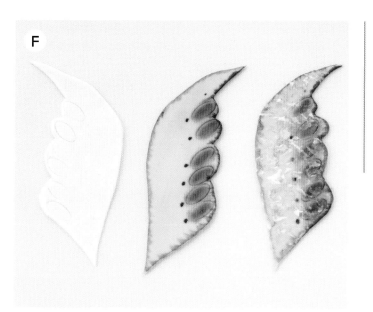

F

Tip

Magic Sparkle Flakes are made from modified starch and are therefore edible. You can attach them with edible glue or clear alcohol.

The fairy . . . .

1 For the lower body roll 10g (⅜oz) of lime green sugarpaste into a cone shape. Take off one third from the widest end of the cone, which will be the top (**G**). Place the pointed end on to the centre of the mushroom and then push a piece of dry spaghetti down through the centre, leaving 4cm (1½in) showing at the top.

2 For the upper body mix 35g (1¼oz) of white sugarpaste with a little chestnut paste food colour to create a flesh tone. Take off 4g (⅛oz) and roll a small cone shape, the point of the cone being the neck. Mould the rest of the cone into the shoulder and chest shape. Cut a straight edge at the base of the shape and apply some glue. Slip the upper body over the spaghetti at the top of the body, easing it carefully through the neck, leaving 2cm (¾in) showing at the top to support the head. Roll a thin lace of lime green sugarpaste and attach this around the body, making a neat join at the back (**G**). Push a short piece of dry spaghetti into each shoulder.

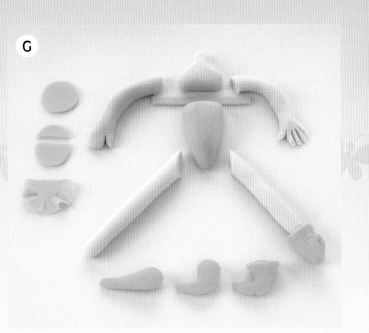

G

3 For the legs you will need 12g (½oz) of the flesh-coloured sugarpaste equally divided. Roll into two thin sausage shapes tapering at one end and make a diagonal cut at the top (**G**). Attach the diagonal cut to each side of the body and bend each leg at the knee, crossing one leg over the other.

4 For the boots make 24g (⅞oz) of turquoise sugarpaste by mixing white with turquoise paste food colour. Take off 4g (⅛oz) and divide it equally to make two small boots. Roll into two small pointed cone shapes, and then turn up the points. Push the back of the cones forwards to make the boot shapes (**G**). Insert the pointed end of tool no.3 into the top of each boot to hollow it out. Thin the edges with your finger, and then apply some edible glue inside the boots, slipping them over the pointed end of each leg.

5 For the skirt roll out the remaining turquoise sugarpaste and cut out one 5cm (2in) circle and one 4cm (1½in) circle. Using a 2cm (¾in) round cutter, take out the centre of each circle. Frill the edges using a cocktail stick or frilling tool (**H**). Slip the largest frill over the body and arrange around the waist and over the legs. Then add the smaller frill over the top. Support the frill until dry using small pieces of foam.

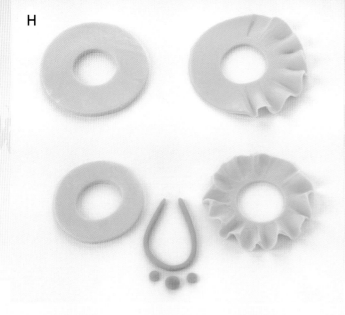

H

Tip

When making frills, dust the work surface liberally with icing (confectioner's) sugar before you begin. This will allow you to move the frill around easily and prevent it sticking. Do not press too hard, just gently roll backwards and forwards on the edge.

6 For the arms you will need 8g (¼oz) of the flesh-coloured sugarpaste equally divided. Roll into two sausage shapes, and then flatten the ends making wooden spoon shapes (**G**). Cut out the thumbs, and then divide the hands into four fingers. Using your finger and thumb take off the square edges, gently rolling each one in between your finger and thumb (**G**). Mark the fingernails by pressing the end of a piece of dry spaghetti into the end of each finger. Narrow the wrists slightly and bend at the elbow.

7 Make a diagonal cut at the top of each arm and attach to the body. Attach the right arm at the shoulder and allow the hand to rest on the knee of the left leg. Complete the left arm as the right, but push a short piece of dry spaghetti from the elbow through the forearm. Allow the end of the spaghetti to push into the left leg to give it support. Arrange the hand into an open position.

8 Make two small frilled sleeves using 1g (⅛oz) of lime green sugarpaste. Cut out two 2cm (¾in) circles. Make a straight cut at the top of the circle and frill the remainder as described for the skirt (**G**). Place the sleeve over the join at the shoulder.

9 Make a tiny butterfly using a 1.5cm (½in) cutter and decorate as described on pages 61–62. Apply some edible glue to the open hand and place the butterfly on the top.

10 Make a necklace for the fairy using 1g (⅛oz) of Lincoln green sugarpaste. Roll out a thin lace and attach around the neck, making a join at the back. Roll one larger ball and flatten with your finger for the centre of the necklace, and a small ball on either side (**H**). Attach with edible glue to the thin lace and add a few Magic Sparkle Flakes (see page 67) over the top.

11 To make the head roll 10g (⅜oz) of the flesh-coloured sugarpaste into a ball, add a small oval shape for the nose in the centre of the face. Make two pointed ears by rolling small cones. Attach to the sides of the head, and then push the end of your paintbrush inside to secure. Add two balls of Lincoln green sugarpaste for the earrings. Roll two small white balls for the eyes and place just above and on either side of the nose (**I**).

12 For the face mix together some purple dust food colour with clear alcohol and, using a no.00 paintbrush, begin to paint a line on either side of the nose, taking it up and over the eyes in an arch. Add the pupils, and then paint a fine line all around the eyes to highlight, then add the eyelashes. Using pink dust food colour mixed with clear alcohol and a no.00 paintbrush, make two dots below the nose to indicate the top lip and one dot below to mark the centre of the lower lip. Make a curved line through the centre. Connect the dots and fill in the lips with pink (**I**).

13 To finish the face add two white dots to highlight the eyes, by dipping the end of a cocktail stick into white paste food colour. Dust the cheeks with pink dust food colour on a dry brush. Slip the head over the spaghetti at the neck and tilt into position.

14 To attach the wings make some stiff glue by mixing sugarpaste with edible glue. Apply the mixture to the edge of the wings and to the back of the body. You may need to support the wings with foam until they have dried in place.

15 For the hair apply a layer of edible glue around the head, and then fill the cup of a sugar press (or garlic press) with 10g (⅜oz) of the remaining light brown sugarpaste softened with white vegetable fat (shortening). Extrude lengths of hair and give the press a shake to keep the strands separate. Lay the press down on to the work surface, and using tool no.4, remove three or four strands at a time and arrange over the head. Start at the back so that the hair falls in between the wings. Attach some of the hair to the wings as this will make them more secure. Continue to layer the hair around the sides of the head, and finally arrange it to the front. Push two gold flower stamens into the top of the head to finish.

A Little More Fun!

Tiny Toadstools

The toadstools from the main cake can be used as a design for these cute mini cakes for all the fairy princesses to take home from the party. Make them in sponge using 5cm (2in) round Silverwood cake pans (see Suppliers, page 126). When the cakes come out of the tins, put them into the freezer so that they can be narrowed at the top. Coat them with buttercream (see page 26) before covering them with sugarpaste and decorating them with motifs from the main cake such as caterpillars, fairy boots and flowers.

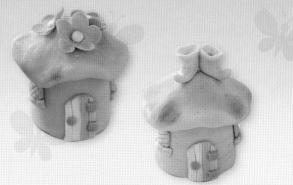

Ballerina Mice

No wonder the mice are dancing – who wouldn't with all this delicious Swiss cheese around? While the mice are busy with the cheese, the cats have their eyes on the mice. Will this be their last encore? This is the perfect cake for a girl's birthday, or perhaps to congratulate a young dancer's success.

"I'm warming up to be the best dancer in the troupe!"

Sugarpaste

★ 750g (1lb 10½oz) yellow
★ 500g (1lb 1½oz) pale blue
★ 270g (9½oz) white
★ 42g (1½oz) mid-brown
★ 12g (½oz) dark blue
★ 9g (⅜oz) pink
★ 6g (¼oz) black
★ 5g (¼oz) peach
★ 5g (¼oz) lilac
★ 3g (⅛oz) green
★ 1g (⅛oz) brown

Materials

★ 20cm (8in) round cake
★ Magic Sparkle Dust in blue, green, crystal, lilac and peach
★ White paste food colour
★ Edible glue (see page 26)
★ Non-toxic glue

Equipment

★ 25cm (10in) petal-shaped cake drum
★ 15cm (6in) cake cards
★ 4cm (1½in), 2.5cm (1in), 2cm (¾in), 1.5cm (½in) round cutters
★ 1.5cm (½in) and 1cm (⅜in) blossom cutters
★ 18 flower stamens
★ Sugar press (or garlic press)
★ Frilling tool (or cocktail stick)
★ Rice-textured rolling pin
★ Blue ribbon 15mm (½in) wide x 1m (40in) long
★ Basic tool kit (see pages 12–13)

Covering the board and cake . . . .

1 To cover the board roll out 500g (1lb 1½oz) of pale blue sugarpaste to an even 5mm (⅛in) thickness. Cover the board in the usual way (see page 30) then run over the surface with a rice-textured rolling pin. Trim the edges of the board using a sharp knife, and then smooth the edges with your finger. Save the off-cuts for use later. Edge the board with the ribbon, securing it with non-toxic glue.

2 Prepare the cake, but first use a sharp knife to carve the edges to make them rounded and smooth just like a cheese. Then use a teaspoon to make some small holes in the cake and use a melon scoop for a few larger holes.

3 To cover the cake roll out 600g (1lb 5oz) of yellow sugarpaste to no less than 5mm (⅛in) thickness. Place the sugarpaste carefully over the top of the cake and find the holes with your finger. Smooth the sugarpaste into the holes as you continue to cover the cake. Trim the edges neatly and save the off-cuts for use later.

4 Once the cake is covered, make some smaller holes in the surface using the rounded end of a wooden spoon, pushing it gently into the sugarpaste, being careful not to break the surface. Trim around the edges neatly and tuck any sugarpaste underneath the cake to make a rounded appearance. Secure the cake to the centre of the board with strong edible glue (see tip page 26).

The cheese-slice screens

To make the screens you will need 150g (5¼oz) of yellow sugarpaste, rolled out to a 5mm (⅛in) thickness. Cut out two rectangular shapes measuring 10 x 8cm (4 x 3⅛in). Place them down on to a flat surface. Using 2.5cm (1in), 2cm (¾in) and 1.5cm (½in) round cutters, cut out some holes in the screens. Save the cut-out pieces for use later. Push a length of dry spaghetti into each side of the screens (**A**). Set aside to dry for 12 hours turning them over halfway through the drying time.

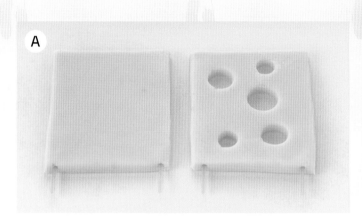

A

The hanging clothes

1 To make the socks roll 1g (⅛oz) of lilac sugarpaste into a thin sausage shape. Turn up at each end to make the foot. Cut in half and using tool no.12, mark the toes and heels with stitch marks (**B**). Attach to the screens with edible glue before they are assembled.

2 Make a coat hanger using 0.5g (⅛oz) of brown sugarpaste rolled into a very small sausage shape. Make an even thinner sausage and attach to the centre for the hook (**B**). Attach the hanger to the top of the screen.

3 To make the ballet dress you will need 3g (⅛oz) of pink sugarpaste. Take off 2g (⅛oz) and roll into a small cone shape. Make a straight cut across the top of the bodice. Roll the remainder into a strip measuring 1 x 5cm (⅜ x 2in) and then frill the edges with a frilling tool (or cocktail stick). Cut the frill in half and attach both parts to the bodice, one on top of the other. Make two small straps and attach to the top of the bodice and over the hanger (**B**).

4 To make the shoes you will need 3g (⅛oz) of white sugarpaste. Take off 2g (⅛oz) and divide equally. Roll into a cone shape then insert the smallest end of tool no.1 into the top to hollow it out. Cut out four thin strips using the remainder of the white sugarpaste and attach to the side of the shoe. Make a bow by folding a short piece in half and gluing the ends together. Roll a small ball and attach to the centre of the bow (**B**). Make two. Place the shoes on to the screen securing with edible glue, and leave to dry.

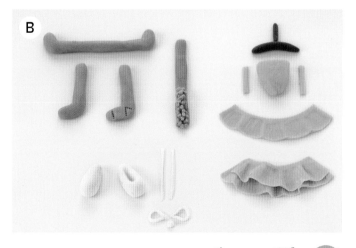

B

Assembling the screen ·

Mix together some CMC/Tylose (see page 9), edible glue and
leftover yellow sugarpaste into a stiff paste. Apply the glue
to the inside edges of the screen. Push the spaghetti on
each section of the screen into the cake, placing the pieces
as close together as you can, and bringing them together
in the middle so they stick. Leave the screen to dry.

The feather boa

To complete the boa you will need 12g (½oz) of dark blue
sugarpaste. Take off 3g (⅛oz) and roll into a strip measuring
1 x 9cm (⅜ x 3½in) and apply a little edible glue to the
strip. Fill the cup of a sugar press (or garlic press) with the
remainder of the blue sugarpaste and extrude very short
lengths of the paste. Chop them off using tool no.4 and
attach to the strip (**B**). Drape over the top of the screen.

The mouse on the right-hand screen ·

1 To complete each mouse you will need 18g (¾oz) of
white sugarpaste mixed together with 1g (⅛oz) of black
to make a pale grey shade. Take off 6g (¼oz) and roll into a
cone shape for a body (**C**). Glue the body into the hole on
the right screen facing the back of the cake.

2 To make the legs take off 4g (⅛oz) and divide equally.
Roll into two cone shapes and bend the feet at the narrow
ends. Flatten a little with your finger, then push a piece of
dry spaghetti into each side of the body and attach the legs.
Add three small pink balls on the end of each foot for the
pads and a small pad in the centre (**C**).

3 For the tail take off 2g (⅛oz) and roll into a sausage
shape. Twist it and then attach to the back of the mouse (**C**).

Tip
When marking the features with tool no.4,
place the point on the table to indent the
lines, do not drag the tool downwards.

C

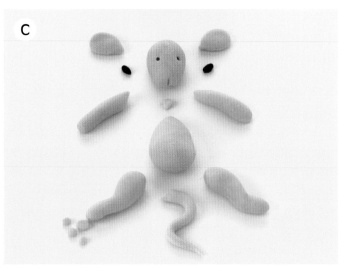

The mouse on the left-hand screen

1 For the head take off 6g (¼oz) and roll into a cone shape. Using tool no.4, mark the centre front of the head with a line (**C**), and then make a diagonal line coming from each side for the mouth. Glue the head into a hole on the left screen.

2 For the ears equally divide 1g (⅛oz) and roll into two cone shapes. Flatten the cones with your finger and attach to either side of the head. Add two small oval shapes of black sugarpaste for the eyes, and a small pink nose (**C**).

3 For the paw roll a small ball in grey sugarpaste and glue into a smaller hole next to the head. Add a few slivers of cheese made from the off-cuts of the screen to the top of the cake, and then glue one to the mouth of the mouse.

The cat on the cake

1 To complete the two cats randomly mix together 46g (1⅝oz) of white sugarpaste with 42g (1½oz) of mid-brown and 2g (⅛oz) of black to create a marbled effect. Allow 1g (⅛oz) of pink for both cats. For each body, take off 17g (½oz) and roll into a fat cone shape (**D**). Push a short piece of dry spaghetti into the cake where the cat is to be positioned. Apply some edible glue and slip the body over the spaghetti. Push two short pieces of dry spaghetti into the body where the back legs are to be positioned.

2 To make the back legs take off 8g (¼oz) and divide equally. Roll into two cone shapes and narrow at the ankle area. Turn the feet up at the end (**D**) and a slip over the spaghetti. Attach the feet to the side of the cake. For the pads underneath the feet, roll two small pink balls and flatten them, then attach one to each foot.

3 For the front legs take off 6g (¼oz) and roll into a fat sausage shape. Make a diagonal cut in the centre to make two legs. Using tool no.4, mark the paws (**D**) and attach to the front of the body.

4 To make the head take off 9g (⅜oz), roll into a ball and then make it slightly oval shaped (**D**). Push a short piece of dry spaghetti into the centre.

5 For the face take off 1g (⅛oz) of the marbled sugarpaste and divide equally. Roll into two balls and place on either side of the spaghetti. Add a small pink oval shape for the nose and place it over the spaghetti. Roll a small pink ball for the tongue and place this below the nose (**D**).

6 For the ears equally divide 1g (⅛oz) of sugarpaste and roll into two cone shapes. Flatten the cones with your finger and make a straight cut at the widest end (**D**). Apply some edible glue to the head and attach the ears on either side. Push tool no.1 inside the ears to secure them.

7 For the tail take 2g (⅛oz) and roll into a thin tapered sausage shape (**D**). Attach to the back of the cat bringing the end of the tail to the side of the cake.

8 For the eyes roll two small balls of white sugarpaste and attach just above and on either side of the nose. Add a tiny black ball for the pupil on the top of each eye. Make a small banana shape for the eyelid using the body colour and cover the top of each eye (**D**). Direct the eyes towards the mice on the screen.

9 For the hair and whiskers add three small cone shapes in between the cat's ears. Cut three flower stamens in half and push three pieces into each cheek.

10 For the pads roll 12 tiny balls in pink and attach three to each paw (**D**).

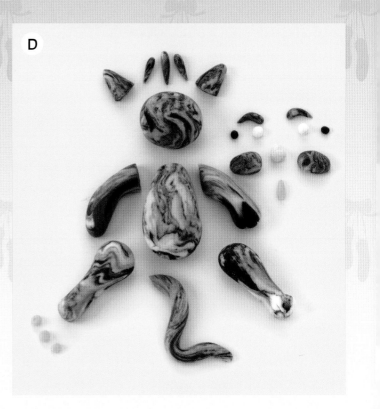

The cat on the board

Make as for the cat on the cake (**D**), but for the body, push the back of the cone upwards so that the body is slightly lifted. Place the front legs stretched out and the back legs in a bent position. Secure the completed cat to the board looking upwards towards where the peach ballerina will be.

Tip

There are several different thicknesses of stamens to choose from. You will find the very fine ones are difficult to push into the sugarpaste without bending them.

The blue ballerina

1 **To complete all the ballerina mice** you will need 100g (3½oz) of grey sugarpaste. To make this, mix together 98g (3½oz) of white sugarpaste with 2g (⅛oz) of black.

2 Make this mouse on a cake card and attach to the top of the cake when complete. Roll 10g (⅜oz) of white sugarpaste into a cone shape for the body. Take off one-third at the top of the cone (**E**). Push a piece of dry spaghetti down through the body leaving 4cm (1½in) showing at the top.

3 **Make the upper body** using 3g (⅛oz) of grey sugarpaste rolled into a small cone shape. Flatten slightly with your finger and shape the shoulders (**E**). Apply some edible glue to the top of the body and slip over the spaghetti at the neck. Mold the two parts together, then roll a small band of white sugarpaste and place this across the chest to cover the join of the upper and lower body, and join neatly at the back.

3 **Make the ballet shoes** using 3g (⅛oz) of white sugarpaste equally divided and rolled into oval shapes (**E**).

4 **For the legs** take off 6g (¼oz) of grey sugarpaste and roll into a sausage shape. Cut into two (**E**) and push a piece of dry spaghetti right down through the leg from the top and into the shoe, securing the two together with edible glue. Attach the body over the top of the legs.

5 **Make the leg warmers** by rolling out 1g (⅛oz) of the pale blue sugarpaste leftover from covering the board into a strip measuring 3 x 1cm (1¼ x ⅜in). Turn over the top edge (**E**) and apply some glue to the back. Place around the ankle of the mouse and join at the back. Make two.

6 **To make the tail** take off 2g (⅛oz) of grey sugarpaste and roll into a tapered cone shape (**E**). Attach to the back of the body. If possible, leave the mouse at this stage to harden off before you begin to dress it.

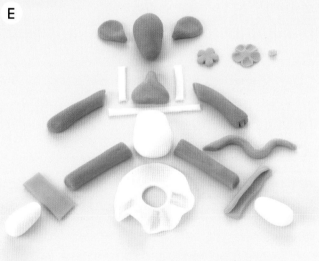

E

7 To make the two skirts you will need 6g (¼oz) of white sugarpaste rolled out and cut into two 4cm (1½in) circles. Dust the work surface with icing (confectioners') sugar and, using a frilling tool (or cocktail stick), begin to frill the edge of the circles. Cut out the centre using a 2cm (¾in) round cutter (**E**). Apply some edible glue very sparingly around the edge of each skirt and add some blue Magic Sparkle Dust with a dry brush. Apply some edible glue around the hips and waist of the mouse and slip the two skirts over the top. Make sure they are both attached to the body all around the waistline.

8 To make the arms take off 4g (⅛oz) of grey sugarpaste and roll into a sausage shape. Make a diagonal cut in the centre and mark the paws at the rounded end using tool no.4. Push a short piece of dry spaghetti into the shoulders and slip the right arm over, securing with edible glue. Bend the arm so that it rests on the hip. Set the left arm aside and keep it covered. Cut a thin strip of white sugarpaste to make a shoulder strap (**E**). Glue over the shoulder to hide the join.

9 For the head roll 6g (¼oz) of grey sugarpaste into a cone shape (**E**). Take tool no.4 and mark the front with a line in the centre. Make a diagonal line on either side to mark the mouth. Push a piece of dry spaghetti into the centre to open the mouth a little. Roll two small black balls for the eyes and glue into position on either side of the head. Add a small white highlight into each eye with some white paste food colour on the end of a cocktail stick.

10 For the ears take off 2g (⅛oz) and divide equally. Roll into two cone shapes and flatten with your fingers. Pinch the narrow ends in a little and attach to each side of the head (**E**).

11 Make the flowers by rolling out 1g (⅛oz) of the leftover pale blue sugarpaste and cuting out two shapes using 1.5cm (½in) and 1cm (⅜in) blossom cutters. Open each petal by rolling it using the end of your paintbrush. Place the smaller blossom on top of the larger one and add a dot of leftover yellow sugarpaste into the centre (**E**). Attach to the head of the mouse. Apply some glue to the top of the body and slip the completed head over the top.

Tip
Place the head into a flower former to prevent it from going flat while you work on it.

12 To make the whiskers cut three flower stamens in half and push three pieces into each side of the face.

13 Attach the left arm and bring the paw up to the mouth area. Cut another thin strip to make the second shoulder strap (**E**) and glue over the shoulder to hide the join.

14 Secure the completed ballerina to the top of the cake looking in the direction of the cat on the cake. Dust the shoes and flowers with blue Magic Sparkle Dust.

The green ballerina

Make the body in the same way as the blue ballerina and place on to a cake card. Attach the legs, placing one in front and one behind the body as if doing the splits. Complete as described on pages 79–80, using 3g (⅛oz) of green sugarpaste for the leg warmers and flowers. Attach the right arm to the head and the left arm down at the side. Dust the edge of the skirt the shoes and flowers with green Magic Sparkle Dust. Position the completed ballerina on top of the cake in front of the blue ballerina, securing with edible glue.

The pink ballerina

Construct exactly as for the blue ballerina (see pages 79–80), but position the arms together at the front of the body. Use 3g (⅛oz) of pink sugarpaste for the leg warmers and flowers. Dust the edge of the skirt, the shoes and flowers with crystal Magic Sparkle Dust.

Tip

When using the Magic Sparkle Dust, ensure you dust it on to freshly modelled paste so that it sticks – if you dust it on to a dry surface it will just blow away.

The lilac ballerina

1 Make the ballerina as described on pages 79–80 but only attach the left leg. You will only need 17g (½oz) of white sugarpaste for this mouse as the shoes are made in lilac, but the leg warmers are made in white. Allow 3g (⅛oz) of lilac sugarpaste for the shoes and 1g (⅛oz) for the flowers.

2 Position the arms as shown and bring the tail around the back of the body and through the arm to the front. Set the ballerina aside. Bend the right leg slightly at the knee and attach to the side of the cake at the correct height of the body, and then place the mouse next to it, lifting the skirt over the top of the leg. Dust the shoes, flowers and the edge of the skirt with lilac Magic Sparkle Dust.

The peach ballerina

1 To complete this ballerina you will need 12g (½oz) of white sugarpaste and 5g (¼oz) of peach. Roll 6g (¼oz) of white sugarpaste into a ball. Apply some edible glue into the hole at the side of the cake and push a piece of dry spaghetti into it. Slip the ball over the top. Push a short piece of spaghetti into the ball to support the tail.

2 Cut out two skirts and frill them as described on page 80. Place the skirts over the ball and secure to the side of the cake with edible glue.

3 Make the tail by rolling 2g (⅛oz) of grey sugarpaste into a tapered cone and slip over the spaghetti.

4 Make the legs using 6g (¼oz) of grey sugarpaste rolled into a sausage shape, then divide in the centre. Turn up the ends to form the feet and make them a little pointed. Bend at the knee then push a short piece of dry spaghetti into the end of each leg and push into the side of the body, with the feet upturned. Use 2g (⅛oz) of peach sugarpaste to make the leg warmers and attach around the ankles as before.

5 For the shoes take 3g (⅛oz) of peach sugarpaste, divide equally and roll into oval shapes, then push tool no.1 gently into the tops to hollow them out. Place the shoes on the board and dust with peach Magic Sparkle Dust.

A Little More Fun!

Ballet Buns

Cheese is the order of the day as these heavenly smelling cup cakes (see page 24) are iced with delicious cream cheese frosting. To make this, follow the buttercream recipe on page 26 but replace half the butter with cream cheese. Decorate the tops with a pair of ballet shoes, a feather boa or even a chunk of sugarpaste Swiss cheese! With all these mice around, will there be any left for your guests?

Halloween Magic

The good witch is busy casting spells in her magical cauldron, while her cat is distracted by a particularly wriggly spider. This cake is fairly simple to make but has maximum impact, and would be the perfect end to a fun night's trick-or-treating or a children's Halloween party.

"My mistress needs a spider for her magic spell ... come here!"

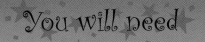

You will need

Sugarpaste

★ 670g (1lb 7⅝oz) orange
★ 470g (1lb ½oz) dark green
★ 130g (4½oz) mid-brown
★ 40g (1½oz) black
★ 35g (1¼oz) white
★ 35g (1¼oz) pink
★ 20g (¾oz) dark blue
★ 16g (½oz) peach
★ 10g (⅜oz) brown
★ 9g (⅜oz) lilac
★ 2g (⅛oz) yellow

Materials

★ 20cm (8in) petal-shaped cake
★ Blue Magic Sparkle Flakes
★ Magic Sparkle Dust
★ Sapphire and Jade Moon
   Beams Dust
★ Dust food colour in dark
   brown, chestnut and pink
★ Paste food colour in bright
   green and violet
★ 8g (¼oz) sugar flower paste
   (see page 25)
★ White vegetable fat
   (shortening)
★ Edible glue (see page 26)
★ Non-toxic glue

Equipment

★ 30cm (12in) petal-shaped
   cake drum
★ FMM cobbles impression mat
★ 1cm (⅜in) star cutter
★ 1cm (⅜in) wide flat brush
★ 1.5cm (½in) blossom cutter
★ 5cm (2in) and 4cm (1½in)
   round cutters
★ 3 white flower stamens
★ Metallic blue florists' wire
★ Dark green ribbon 15mm
   (½in) wide x 1m (40in) long
★ Basic tool kit (see pages 12–13)

Covering the board and cake . . . .

1 To cover the board roll out 375g (13¼oz) of dark green sugarpaste to an even thickness of 3mm (⅛in). Cover the board in the usual way (see page 30) and trim around the edges neatly. Edge the board with the ribbon, securing it with non-toxic glue.

2 To cover the cake, first prepare it then roll out 600g (1lb 5oz) of orange sugarpaste and cover in the usual way (see page 28). As this is a petal shaped cake, be sure to smooth the paste into the sides, keeping the shape of the cake. Secure the cake to the board with strong edible glue, positioning it just off-centre and leaving a little extra room at the front.

The cobbles

1 Make the cobbles for the top of the cake using 100g (3½oz) of mid-brown sugarpaste rolled out to a 3mm (⅛in) thickness. Place the impression mat over the top and press it firmly with your hand. Run the rolling pin over the top and then lift the mat carefully.

2 Make the edge of the cobbles an irregular shape by cutting around the outline of the cobbles with a sharp knife, then soften the edges with your finger (**A**). Attach the cobbles with edible glue to the top of the cake.

3 Dust the top with a 1cm (⅜in) wide brush and some dark brown dust food colour (**A**).

4 Using the same brush, dust inside the vertical lines down the side of the cake, and around the top of the cake to make it look more like a pumpkin.

The broomstick

1 To complete the broomstick you will need 30g (1oz) of mid-brown sugarpaste. Take off 4g (⅛oz) for the handle and roll into a thin sausage shape measuring 9cm (3½in) long (**A**). Push a length of dry spaghetti through the handle, leaving 3cm (1¼in) showing at the end.

2 Make the head and the bristles by rolling 3g (⅛oz) of the sugarpaste into a half-moon shape. Using tool no.4 mark a line along the straight edge and glue the other edge to the handle. Add some white vegetable fat (shortening) to the remainder of the sugarpaste and fill the cup of the sugar press (or garlic press). Extrude strands and chop them off, apply some edible glue and attach to the broom head.

3 Mark the top of the handle with two lines using tool no.4 (**A**). Attach the broomstick to the top of the cake in front of the cobbles. The end of the handle should be just over the edge of the centre of the cake.

Tip
Twist the dry spaghetti gently as you insert it through a long length of sugarpaste.

The cauldron

1 To make the pot take 60g (2oz) of dark green sugarpaste, roll it into a ball then push the end of a small rolling pin inside the ball to hollow it out. Continue to shape and mould the pot with your fingers, pinching around the top to form a rim (**B**).

2 To make the handle roll 1g (⅛oz) of dark green sugarpaste into a sausage shape and cut in half. Indent all around by gently rolling a piece of spaghetti on the surface one-third from the end. Flatten this end with your finger to shape (**B**). Push a short piece of dry spaghetti into the side of the pot and slip the handle over. Place the pot inside a flower former (or similar) to hold the shape until it dries.

3 Fill the inside of the cauldron three-quarters full with 5g (¼oz) of dark blue sugarpaste rolled into balls. Roll a further 5g (¼oz) of the same sugarpaste into a ball and flatten with your hand. Pinch the surface all over with your fingers to make it look waves (**B**), and then place it over the top of the balls inside the pot.

4 Apply a very light coat of edible glue to the surface, and then sprinkle some blue Magic Sparkle Flakes over the top. Shake off any excess. Dust the outside of the cauldron with Sapphire Moon Beams Dust. Place the cauldron on top of the cake and secure to the cobbles with edible glue.

5 To make the logs around the pot you will need 10g (⅜oz) of brown sugarpaste. Take off 6g (¼oz) and make a sausage shape long enough to go around the bottom of the pot – approximately 16cm (6¼in) long. Flatten slightly with your finger and, using tool no.4, mark to look like bark. Attach around the base of the pot with edible glue. Make some shorter logs to place around the pot too (**B**).

6 To make the flames take 3g (⅛oz) of orange sugarpaste and divide into eight small cone shapes. Press them to flatten slightly with your finger and then, using tool no.4, mark vertical lines to look like flames (**B**). Secure around the logs with edible glue.

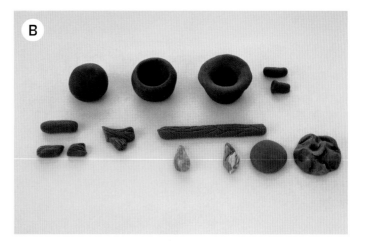

Tip

When making the flames, you could marble together 1g (1/8oz) of yellow sugarpaste and 2g (1/8oz) of orange to create a more dramatic fiery effect (B).

The star burst

1 Cut three lengths of metallic blue flower wire into two. Twist the lengths around a cake dowel in the centre of the wire, leaving the ends straight (**C**).

2 Make three purple stars using 1g (⅛oz) of sugar flower paste coloured with violet paste food colour, also make one star using white and two stars using dark blue sugarpaste (**C**). Apply some glue to the back of each star and press the ends of the wires into them. Secure the stars with a dot of the same coloured sugarpaste then push the wires into the top of the cauldron.

The witch

1 **For the shoes** add some bright green paste food colour to 16g (½oz) of white sugarpaste and knead well to disperse the colour. Take off 6g (¼oz) and divide equally. Roll into two sausage shapes and narrow slightly in the middle. Using the end of your paintbrush, hollow out at the top where the legs are to be inserted (**D**).

2 **For the soles of the shoes** equally divide 3g (⅛oz) of dark green sugarpaste. Roll into two sausage shapes and flatten with your finger. Attach with edible glue to the base of the shoes, turning the soles upwards at the toes.

3 **Make the legs** using 2g (⅛oz) of yellow sugarpaste rolled into a sausage shape measuring 4cm (1½in) long. Cut in half (**D**) and push a length of dry spaghetti through the centre of each leg, leaving 2cm (¾in) showing at the top and bottom. Apply some edible glue inside the shoes and push the legs and spaghetti firmly into them.

4 **Make the frills** to go over the top of the legs using 2g (⅛oz) of dark blue sugarpaste. Cut out two blossom shapes. Using the end of your paintbrush, roll the edge of each petal to open it up (**D**). Apply some edible glue to the top of the legs and slip the frills over the spaghetti.

5 **For the lower body** randomly mix together 9g (⅜oz) of pink, dark blue, bright green and lilac sugarpaste making 36g (1¼oz) in total. Roll into a smooth ball (**D**) then divide it at the base to form two sections. Roll the sharp edges with your finger to soften them, then push the spaghetti showing at the top of the legs into each section.

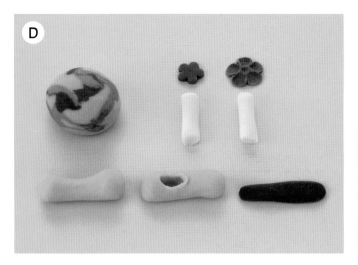

D

Tip

Make sure that the legs are straight and the body is kept upright. If necessary support it at the back with foam until dry.

6 To make the skirt of the coat roll out 10g (⅜oz) of pink sugarpaste and then cut out a 5cm (2in) circle. Take out a 'V' shape at the front (**E**) and attach centrally over the top of the body.

7 Shape the upper body using 4g (⅛oz) of peach sugarpaste rolled into a small cone shape. Using your finger, narrow the neck and shape the shoulders (**E**). Push a piece of dry spaghetti down through the neck and out at the other end.

8 Make the bust by equally dividing 3g (⅛oz) of peach sugarpaste and rolling into two balls (**E**). Push two short pieces of dry spaghetti into the chest and attach the balls with edible glue.

9 For the upper part of the coat roll out 6g (¼oz) of pink sugarpaste into a strip measuring 3 x 10cm (1¼ x 4in) (**E**). Apply some edible glue all around the body and place the strip in the centre front of the torso. Wrap the strip around to join at the back and trim neatly.

10 Make a small cut at the front of the bodice and turn over to make a collar. Mould the jacket to fit the figure snuggly. Apply some edible glue to the base and attach to the lower body pushing the spaghetti into it to secure.

11 Add some buttons in dark blue sugarpaste to the front of the jacket. Add two small squares of bright green sugarpaste for patches on the jacket, and stitch mark around them with tool no.12 (**E**).

12 To make the sleeves you will need 6g (¼oz) of pink sugarpaste equally divided and rolled into two tapered cone shapes (**E**). Push the pointed end of tool no.3 into the widest end to hollow it out slightly.

13 Attach the arms at the shoulder in a bent position. To support the arm, ensure that the elbow is resting on the body, so that you can push a piece of dry spaghetti down from the wrist area through the elbow and anchor it into the hip. Leave some spaghetti showing at the widest end of the sleeves to support the hands.

14 For the hands take 2g (⅛oz) of peach sugarpaste and divide equally. Make two small cone shapes and flatten with your finger. Cut out the thumbs and mark the remainder of the hands into four fingers. Gently roll and pull each finger to take off the edges (**E**). Add the nails by pressing some dry spaghetti into the end of the fingers and thumbs. Slip the hands over the spaghetti at the end of the sleeves. Arrange the hands with the palms outwards.

15 To complete the head you will need 7g (¼oz) of peach sugarpaste. Take off 6g (¼oz) and roll into a small cone shape. Push a short piece of dry spaghetti into the centre of the face, and then roll a short sausage shape for the nose. Attach the nose in a hooked position, securing with edible glue. Using tool no.11, add a smile under the nose (**E**).

16 Roll two small cone shapes for the ears. Using the end of your paintbrush, indent the base of the cone to attach the ear to the side of the head. For the eyes, roll two tiny round balls in white sugarpaste, and add two much smaller balls of brown sugarpaste for the pupils (**E**). Dust the cheeks with pink dust food colour on a dry brush.

The hat and hair

1 **Make the hat** using 8g (¼oz) of sugar flower paste coloured with violet paste food colour. Cut out a 4cm (1½in) circle and take out a 1cm (⅜in) circle from the centre (**F**); this will help the hat fit the top of the head.

2 Roll the remaining flower paste into a tall cone shape. Push a short piece of dry spaghetti into the top of the head. Twist the cone (**F**) then apply some edible glue around the spaghetti and attach the hat.

3 Roll out 1g (⅛oz) of white sugarpaste and cut out a star. Attach the star to the front of the hat. Dust the hat with Magic Sparkle Dust.

4 **For the hair** fill the cup of the sugar press (or garlic press) with 8g (¼oz) of orange sugarpaste softened with white vegetable fat (shortening). Extrude some strands and twist them to make curls (**F**). Apply some edible glue around the head underneath the hat and attach the curls.

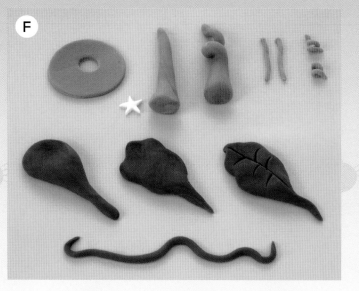

The pumpkin border

1 Take 15g (½oz) of dark green sugarpaste and add to it 15g (½oz) of white sugarpaste to lighten the colour. Roll a lace and form a pattern to decorate the cake like the tendrils and vine of the pumpkin (**F**).

2 **Make a pumpkin leaf** using 3g (⅛oz) of the dark green sugarpaste. Roll into an oval shape, and then make the end very pointed. Mould the shape of the leaf with your fingers. Using tool no.4, mark the veins (**F**). Make two and attach to the board in between the pumpkins.

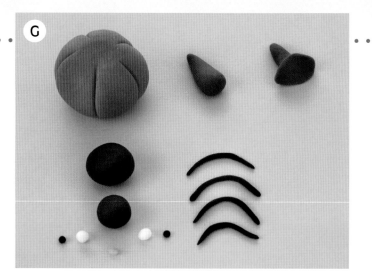

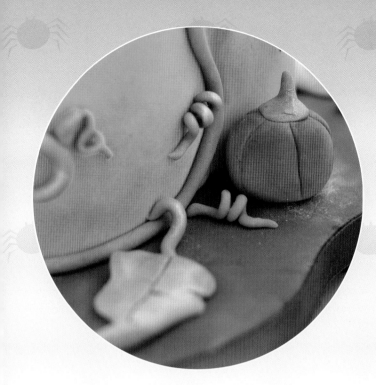

3 For the pumpkins you will need 60g (2oz) of orange sugarpaste. Take off 20g (¾oz) and roll into a ball. Using tool no.4, mark the vertical lines around the pumpkin. Make three. Using 3g (⅛oz) of dark green, add a small stalk to the top of each pumpkin in the shape of a small witch's hat (**G**).

4 Dust around the top of the pumpkins with chestnut dust food colour. Using Jade Moon Beams Dust, dust the stalk on each pumpkin, the vines and tendrils and also round the pumpkins on the board.

The spider

1 To complete the spider you will need 2g (⅛oz) of black sugarpaste. Push a short piece of dry spaghetti into the side of the cake, 3cm (1¼in) below the broom handle. Roll 1g (⅛oz) of black sugarpaste into a ball for the body (**G**). Apply some edible glue around the spaghetti and push the ball over the top.

2 For the head take a smaller amount of black and roll into a ball Attach this to the body. Roll a tiny ball of pink sugarpaste and attach this to the centre front of the head as the nose (**G**). Using tool no.11, add a small smile under the nose.

3 Make the eyes from two small balls of white sugarpaste and attach to the front of the head. Add smaller black pupils on the top (**G**).

4 Roll the remainder of the black sugarpaste into a very thin lace. Cut off a piece long enough to wrap around the broom handle and attach it to the back of the spider. Make four shorter lengths for the legs and glue under the body (**G**). Attach the back legs to the cake to steady the spider.

The black cat

1 To complete the cat you will need 38g (1⅜oz) of black sugarpaste. Take off 15g (½oz) for the body and roll into a fat cone shape (**H**). Place the cone on top of the cake with the pointed end near the edge. Push a short piece of spaghetti into the hip area on either side of the cat.

2 For the back legs take off 8g (¼oz) and divide equally. Roll into two cone shapes keeping the narrowest ends rounded. Using the side of your little finger, gently roll around the ankle area to shape. Using tool no.4, mark the paws (**H**). Apply some edible glue and slip the legs over the spaghetti at the hips.

3 For the front legs equally divide 3g (⅛oz) of black sugarpaste and roll into a long cone shape. Make a diagonal cut in the centre and attach to the body (**G**). Add the paw marks as before then place the right paw over the handle of the broom and the left paw hanging over the side of the cake. Push a short piece of dry spaghetti into the neck area.

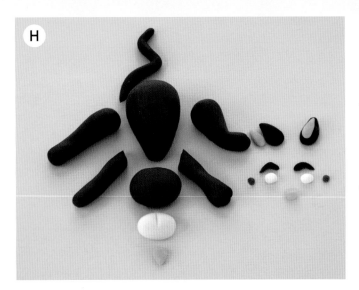

4 For the head roll 6g (¼oz) into a ball, making it slightly oval shaped. Push a piece of dry spaghetti into the centre of the face and then add 2g (⅛oz) of white sugarpaste rolled into a ball over the top. Mark the centre of the ball with a line. Push the end of your paintbrush into the bottom of the line to mark the mouth. Add a tiny pink sugarpaste cone at the top for the nose, and another for the tongue (**H**). Push the tongue into the small hole you have made for the mouth.

5 For the eyes make two small white balls and attach just above and on either side of the nose. Add small green pupils using some of the green leftover from the pumpkin border. Make two small banana shapes in black sugarpaste for the eyebrows (**H**).

6 For the ears make two small cone shapes and flatten slightly with your finger. Roll a tiny teardrop shape in pink sugarpaste and glue on the top of each ear. Flatten again with your finger (**H**). Make a straight cut at the base of each cone and attach to either side of the head, securing with edible glue and tool no.1.

7 Cut three flower stamens in half and push three into each side of the cheeks to make the whiskers. Using 4g (⅛oz) of black sugarpaste, roll a long cone shape for the tail (**H**). Attach to the back of the cat, curling the end over the witch's shoe.

Tip

When working with black sugarpaste, condition your hands with a little white vegetable fat (shortening) first. This will prevent the black pigment from going into your pores and will help keep your hands clean.

A Little More Fun!

Cobblestone Cup Cakes

The perfect treat for anyone who comes calling on Halloween night, these great cup cakes have been decorated with the cobbles made in the same way as on the main cake, but cut into circles using a large round cutter. The witch's hat, pumpkin and spider from the main cake have been used as decorations, but you could also try making other Halloween-themed items such as classic white-sheeted ghosts, cheeky devils and funny monsters.

Cute Christening

The angelic newborn is fast asleep while the big sister and
brother are enjoying welcoming the baby to the family.
The birth of a baby is always a reason to celebrate and
this cake is perfect to mark baby coming home or as
the highlight of the Christening meal.

"It's not fair – the baby is getting more attention than me!"

You will need

Sugarpaste

- ★ 2kg 688g (5lb 14⅞oz) white
- ★ 117g (4⅛oz) flesh
- ★ 98g (3½oz) yellow
- ★ 53g (1⅞oz) blue
- ★ 29g (1oz) pink
- ★ 19g (¾oz) red
- ★ 12g (½oz) dark brown
- ★ 10g (⅜oz) light brown
- ★ 1g (⅛oz) black

Materials

- ★ 30 x 25cm (12 x 10in) oval cake
- ★ 15 x 10cm (6 x 4in) oval cake
- ★ Pink dust food colour
- ★ White paste food colour
- ★ Liquid food colour in brown and buttercup yellow
- ★ White vegetable fat (shortening)
- ★ Edible glue (see page 26)
- ★ Non-toxic glue

Equipment

- ★ 36 x 30cm (14⅛ x 12in) oval cake drum
- ★ 15 x 10cm (6 x 4in) oval cake cards
- ★ 2cm (¾in) flower cutter
- ★ 6cm (2⅜in), 5cm (2in), 1.5cm (½in) and 1cm (⅜in) round cutters
- ★ Straight-edged Garrett frill cutter
- ★ Daisy-textured rolling pin
- ★ Star-shaped modelling tool
- ★ Sugar press (or garlic press)
- ★ White ribbon 15mm (½in) wide x 1m (40in) long
- ★ Basic tool kit (see pages 12–13)

Covering the board and cakes ·············

1 To cover the board and cakes you will need 2kg (4lb 6½oz) of white sugarpaste. Take off 700g (1lb 8⅝oz) to cover the board and roll out to an even 3mm (⅛in) thickness. Cover the board in the usual way (see page 30) and trim the edges neatly keeping the knife vertical. Edge the board with the ribbon, securing with non-toxic glue.

> ### Tip
> You can take out the centre of the sugarpaste on the board just smaller than the cake to save 250g (8¾oz). This will be enough to make the frilled skirt around the crib.

2 To cover the large cake take off a further 1kg (2lb 3¼oz) and roll out to an even 5mm (⅛in) thickness. Prepare the cake and cover in the usual way (see page 28). Trim the edges very neatly and smooth the surface and sides of the cake using smoothers. Attach to the board with strong edible glue (see tip page 26), dowel the cake (see page 31) and set aside to dry.

3 To shape the small cake for crib take a sharp knife and hollow out the top of the cake, make a gentle slope to the centre to a depth of no more than 2.5cm (1in). Leave a 1cm (⅜in) border around the edge of the cake untouched.

4 To cover the small cake use the remaining 300g (10½oz) of white sugarpaste, roll out and cover as for the large cake. Trim the edges as before, and then place this cake on to a cake card, dusted with icing (confectioners') sugar ready to decorate and set aside.

Decorating the large cake ·············

1 To make the flowers roll out 60g (2oz) of white sugarpaste and use the flower cutter to cut out 34 flowers. Attach the flowers evenly around the base of the cake using edible glue, and then add a second row of flowers in between the first row.

2 For the flower centres take 2g (⅛oz) of pink, yellow and blue sugarpaste. Roll a small ball of each colour and place into the centre of the flowers.

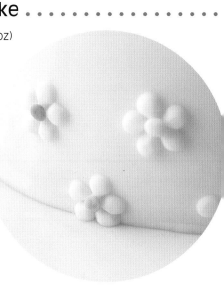

The crib . . . .

1 To make the frilled skirt knead 240g (8½oz) of white sugarpaste with a pinch of CMC (Tylose) to strengthen it (see page 9). Take off 120g (4¼oz) and roll out into a strip measuring 35 x 7.5cm (14 x 3in).

2 Roll over the top of the strip with a daisy-textured rolling pin and then make the edges straight. Slide the handle of your paintbrush under the strip and lift to make some pleats, arranging them so that the piece is long enough to go half way around the crib (**A**).

3 Press the top of the pleated skirt with your finger to hold the folds in place (**A**). Apply some edible glue around the top of the crib and attach the skirt, leaving the remainder to fall free. If necessary, arrange the pleats again with the soft end of your paintbrush before it dries. Repeat for the other side of the crib.

4 To make the frill around the top of the crib you will need 60g (2oz) of white sugarpaste equally divided. Roll out a strip measuring 25 x 1.5cm (10 x ½in), making all the edges straight. Press the straight-edged Garrett frill cutter into the paste, this will mark 13cm (5in), then move the cutter along to make a continuous strip.

5 Using the end of your paintbrush, frill the edges using a backwards and forwards movement. Run a line of stitch marks over the top of the frill with tool no.12 (**B**). Make two. Attach around the top of the crib with edible glue, covering the edge of the skirt.

6 To make the pillow you will need 94g (3⅜oz) of white sugarpaste. Take off 70g (2½oz), roll into a smooth oval shape and flatten to reduce the thickness (**C**). This should fit neatly around the top of the crib.

7 To make the frill around the edge of the pillow use the straight-edged Garrett frill cutter and the remaining 24g (⅞oz) of white sugarpaste. Make the frill to a measurement of 18cm (7in) long, and attach underneath the pillow (**C**). Secure with edible glue to the top of the crib.

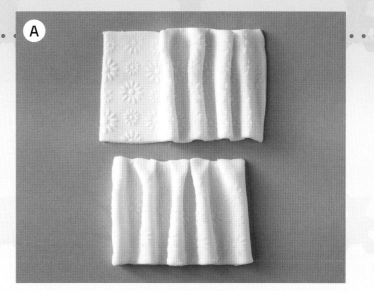

A

Tip

Dust the surface of the sugarpaste with icing (confectioners') sugar to allow the flowers to be removed from the cutter more easily.

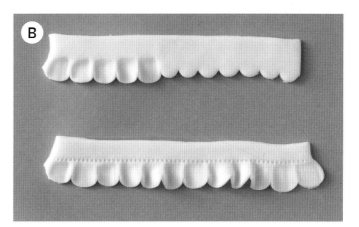

B

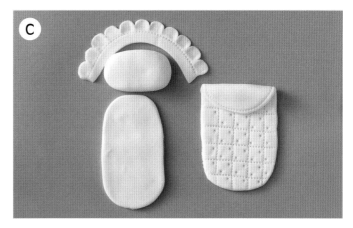

C

The baby

1 For the body roll 36g (1¼oz) of white sugarpaste into a cone shape (**E**), and place this inside the crib with the narrow end resting on the pillow.

2 For the head roll 14g (½oz) of flesh-coloured sugarpaste into a ball then pull down the neck from underneath the ball. Smooth the neck with your fingers. Place the ball into the palm of your hand, and with the side of your little finger on the opposite hand, lightly indent the eye area by rocking it backwards and forwards (**D**).

3 For the nose make a small cone shape and place in the centre of the face, marking two nostrils with tool no.5. Then mark the closed eyes using tool no.11 (**D**).

4 Make the ears from two small cone shapes, attach them to the side of the face and indent at the base with the end of your paintbrush (**D**).

5 For the lips mark the top lip with tool no.4 and the bottom lip with tool no.11. Mark the centre of the lips with tool no.4 (**D**).

6 For the hair take 5g (¼oz) of light brown sugarpaste, make some small, flattened cone shapes and mark the hair using tool no.4. Feather the sugarpaste with the tool to look like fine hair (**D**), and then attach each piece to the head with edible glue. Continue to mark with the tool to define. Repeat the process until the head is covered.

7 For the curl at the top of the head roll a short, feathered piece of hair over your paintbrush to shape it and attach to the top of the head with edible glue.

Tip

Do not use a sugar press to make the baby's hair, as it will be too bulky. Feathering is a better way to achieve finer hair.

8 For the arms roll 2g (¹⁄₁₆oz) of white sugarpaste into a small sausage shape. Make a straight cut at each end, and a diagonal cut in the centre. Push a piece of dry spaghetti into each wrist. Attach at the shoulder of the body with the elbow bent and the wrist facing upwards (**E**).

9 For the hands use 1g (¹⁄₈oz) of flesh-coloured sugarpaste, divided equally. Roll into two cone shapes and flatten with your finger. Cut small 'V' shapes for the thumbs and smooth the edges until they are round. Divide the palms into two, and then into four fingers. Gently roll each finger between until it is rounded. Add fingernails by pressing a piece of dry spaghetti at the end of each finger. Slip the hands over the spaghetti at the wrists (**E**).

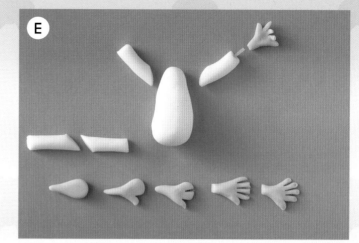

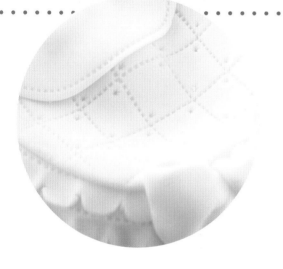

The quilt

1 Roll out 55g (2oz) of white sugarpaste into an oval shape measuring 11 x 9cm (4½ x 3½in). Using tool no.12, stitch mark around the top of the shape and then turn the whole shape over. Stitch mark the main part of the quilt into a square design with vertical and horizontal lines. Mark the top right and bottom left corner of each square with a star-shaped tool (**C**).

2 Turn the top of the quilt over to reveal the stitch marks (**C**) and place it over the baby. Place the crib cake onto the dowels on the large cake before attaching the bow (see below) and secure with edible glue.

The large bow

1 To complete the bow you will need 35g (1¼oz) of white sugarpaste. Take off 23g (⅞oz) and roll out a strip measuring 16 x 4cm (6¼ x 1½in). Cut the strip in half and apply some edible glue to the edge. Fold over to make a loop, and then gently gather the edge. Make two (**F**).

2 For the bow tails roll out the remaining 12g (½oz) of white sugarpaste and cut out a rectangle measuring 8 x 4cm (3⅛ x 1½in). Make a diagonal cut across the strip, and then turn the longest edges facing in. Make a further diagonal cut at the end of the strips to shape the tails (**F**).

3 Attach the tails to the end of the crib and then glue each section of the bow over the top. Cut out a small rectangle to go over the centre of the bow to finish (**F**).

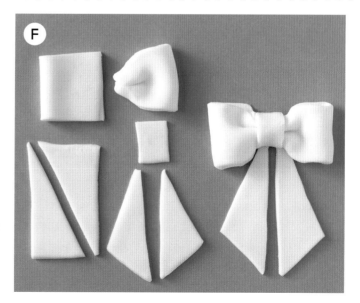

The girl

1 For the legs roll 30g (1oz) of flesh-coloured sugarpaste into a sausage shape 10cm (4in) long. Make a diagonal cut in the centre of the sausage (**G**). Push a length of dry spaghetti through the centre of each leg, leaving 2cm (¾in) showing at the top.

2 For the shoes take 15g (½oz) of red sugarpaste and roll into two oval shapes (**G**). Apply some edible glue to the base of the legs, slip the shoes over the spaghetti and then stand upright.

3 For the socks roll 6g (¼oz) of white sugarpaste into a strip measuring 7 x 3cm (2¾ x 1¼in). Divide the strip into two and then turn over the top edge (**G**). Arrange each strip around the ankle, making a neat join on the inside.

4 For the body roll 30g (1oz) of white sugarpaste into a cone shape (**G**) and gently push the cone on to the dry spaghetti at the top of each leg. Make sure that the cone has good contact, and then stand upright, ensuring the feet are level.

> *Tip*
> *Leave the body and legs to harden overnight before dressing the figure.*

5 To make the petticoat roll out 20g (¾oz) of white sugarpaste into a strip measuring 20 x 3cm (8 x 1¼in). Make the pleats using the end of your paintbrush. Spread the pleats evenly and then press down the top edge to prevent them from moving (**G**). Apply some edible glue around the body and attach the frill, making the join at the front of the body. Lift up the edges of the frill.

6 For the skirt roll out 15g (½oz) of yellow sugarpaste and cut out a 6cm (2⅜in) circle. Roll out 4g (⅛oz) of red sugarpaste thinly and cut out some 1cm (3⅜in) circles. Glue the circles to the skirt, and then roll over the top with a rolling pin. Take out a 1.5cm (½in) circle from the centre (**H**), and slip the skirt over the body. Attach with edible glue around the waistline.

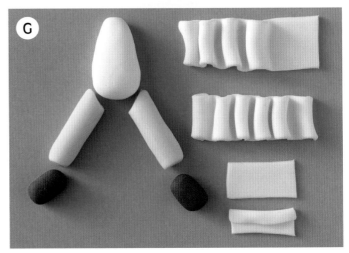

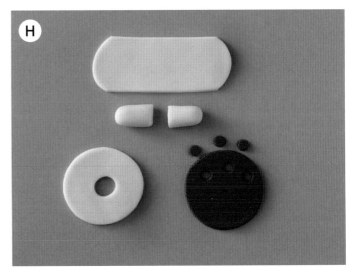

7 For the jacket roll out 14g (½oz) of yellow sugarpaste and cut into a strip measuring 10 x 3cm (4 x 1¼in) and then round off the ends (**H**). Wrap the strip around the top of the body meeting at the front. Turn over at the top edge to form the lapels.

8 For the sleeves roll 8g (¼oz) of yellow sugarpaste into a small sausage shape, and then cut in half to make two sleeves (**H**). Set aside. Stand the figure in the required position at the side of the crib. Push two short pieces of dry spaghetti into the body at the shoulders.

9 To make the arms you will need 8g (¼oz) of flesh coloured sugarpaste equally divided. Roll into two sausage shapes, and then narrow at the wrists. Flatten the end to look like a wooden spoon shape. Cut the thumbs and fingers and shape as described for the baby (see page 101) (**I**). Push a short piece of dry spaghetti into the top of the arms, and then glue on the sleeves.

10 Attach the arms and sleeves to the top of the body over the spaghetti at the shoulders. Apply some edible glue to the palm of the right hand and place over the crib for support. The left elbow is resting on the crib with the hand facing upwards in order to support the teddy bear.

11 For the head roll 17g (½oz) of flesh-coloured sugarpaste into a smooth ball. Pull down the neck from the base of the ball, and indent the eye area with the side of your finger using a rocking movement. Add the nose in the centre of the face, and mark a small hole for the mouth with the end of your paintbrush (**I**).

12 For the eyes make two more holes just above and on either side of the nose. Roll two small white balls and glue them into the holes, and then add much smaller balls of blue sugarpaste on the top. Using a no.000 paintbrush and some brown liquid food colour, paint around the base of the eyes, adding some fine eyelashes. Paint on the eyebrows in a gentle curve (**I**). Add a white highlight to the eyes with some white paste food colour on a cocktail stick.

13 For the lips roll a small ball of flesh-coloured sugarpaste and push this into the mouth hole. Shape with the soft end of your paintbrush to look like lips (**I**).

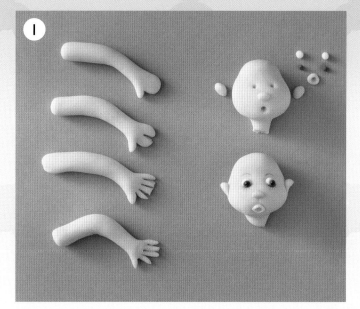

Tip
Place the head inside a flower former while you work on it, as this will help keep its rounded shape.

14 For the ears roll two small cone shapes and attach to the sides of the head, then indent the cones with the end of your paintbrush (**I**).

15 To make the hair soften 10g (⅜oz) of dark brown sugarpaste with white vegetable fat (shortening), and then fill the cup of the sugar press (or garlic press). Extrude the hair to about 3cm (1¼in) and lay the press down on the work surface. Slide tool no.4 through the strands, removing a few at a time. Arrange into the style, starting at the back of the head by layering and finish at the side.

16 For the curls take off three strands and twist together and attach to the side of the head. Add a few thin tapered cone shapes to make a fringe. Add a small white rectangle on each side to make the hair decoration.

17 Dust the cheeks with a dry brush and some pink dust food colour. Apply some edible glue to the neck area and slip the completed head on to the body. Turn the head so that it is looking down towards where the little boy will be.

The teddy bear

1 To complete the bear you will need 13g (½oz) of grey sugarpaste, made by mixing together 1oz (⅛oz) of black with 12g (½oz) of white. Take off 3g (⅛oz) for the body and roll into a cone shape (**J**). Push a piece of dry spaghetti down through the body leaving 5mm (⅛in) showing at the top.

2 For the legs roll a sausage using 4g (⅛oz). Turn up at each end for the feet and make a diagonal cut in the centre (**J**). Attach the diagonal cuts to the body with edible glue.

3 For the arms take off 2g (⅛oz) and roll into a sausage shape, make a diagonal cut again in the centre (**J**). Attach the arms to the top of the body.

4 For the head roll 3g (⅛oz) into a ball and indent the eye area. Push the muzzle up at the front of the face (**J**). Using tool no.12, mark the centre front of the muzzle. Make holes for the mouth and eyes with tool no.5. Roll two small black balls and place into the eyeholes. Make a hole at the top of the muzzle, and then make a small black cone shape for the nose. Glue this into the hole.

5 For the ears roll two small balls (**J**) and attach to the side of the head, securing with tool no.1. Place the completed bear on top of the crib. Apply some edible glue to the palm of the girl's hand and rest the bear against it for support.

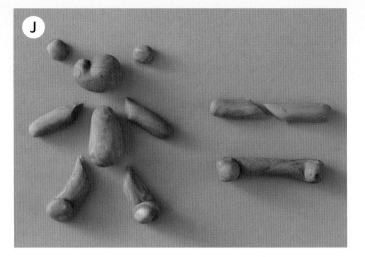

The little boy

1 For the body make a blue cone shape and a yellow cone shape using 22g (¾oz) of sugarpaste for each. Cut the cones in half and then place the top of the yellow cone on to the base of the blue cone (**K**). Push a piece of dry spaghetti down through the two halves. Insert a short piece of dry spaghetti into the shoulder area.

2 To make the trouser legs you will need 24g (⅞oz) of blue sugarpaste equally divided. Roll each into a tapered cone shape, and then insert the end of tool no.3 inside the widest end. This will hollow it out to allow the lower leg to be inserted. Make a diagonal cut at the top of each leg and attach to the body (**K**).

Cute Christening

3 For the legs roll 18g (¾oz) of flesh-coloured sugarpaste into a sausage shape. Turn up the ends to form the feet, as described for the teddy bear (see page 104). Cut in half, and using tool no.4, mark the big toes and then separate them. Take off the sharp edges by rolling in between your finger and thumb.

4 Divide the rest of the foot into two, and then into four making four toes. Roll all the sharp edges to make them soft and round. Using a piece of dry spaghetti, press lightly on the end of each toe to mark the nails (**K**).

5 Push a piece of dry spaghetti into the top of each leg and insert it into the base of the trouser, securing with edible glue. Place the figure on to the side of the cake.

6 For the sleeves roll 6g (¼oz) of yellow sugarpaste into a sausage shape and make a diagonal cut in the centre to form two sleeves (**K**). Set aside.

7 For the arms take 14g (½oz) of flesh-coloured sugarpaste equally divided. Roll into two sausage shapes and complete as described on page 103 (**K**). Attach the arms to the base of the yellow sleeves, and then slip over the spaghetti at the shoulders. Position the arms as shown.

8 To make the bib and braces roll out 2g (⅛oz) of blue sugarpaste. Cut out a small square and attach to the front of the body. Cut two thin straps and glue to the top of the bib, over the shoulders and crossed at the back. Finish with two small heart buttons, made by rolling tiny cones of lighter blue (add some white to the colour you used for the trousers) and use tool no.4 to indent the top of the cones. Soften the raw edges to make them smooth (**K**) and attach to the ends of the straps.

9 For the head you will need 15g (½oz) of flesh-coloured sugarpaste, shaping the head as described on page 103. Mark the mouth with tool no.11 and open it up a little with the soft end of your paintbrush. Add a tiny rectangle of white for the teeth, using tool no.4 to divide the teeth. Add some freckles with a no.000 paintbrush and some brown liquid food colour. When dry, dust the cheeks with a dry brush and some pink dust food colour (**L**).

10 For the hat add 3g (⅛oz) of blue to 6g (¼oz) of white and mix together to make a pale shade. Cut out the brim of the hat using a 5cm (2in) round cutter. Apply some edible glue around the head and arrange the brim. Make the crown of the hat by rolling the remaining light blue sugarpaste into a ball, flatten slightly (**L**) and attach to the top of the head.

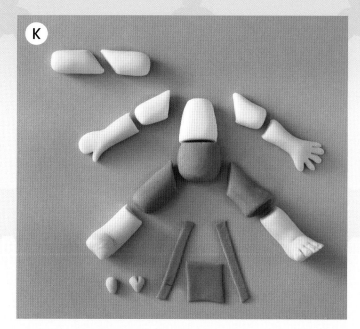

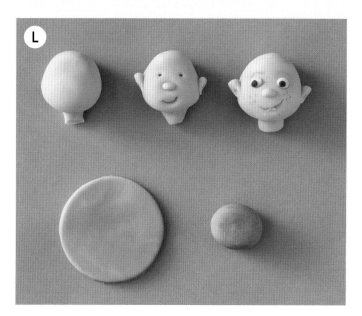

The elephant

1 To complete the elephant you will need 2g (⅛oz) of white sugarpaste and 26g (1oz) of yellow. Take off 5g (¼oz) of yellow sugarpaste and roll into a ball, then flatten the ball with your finger to form a circular body shape (**M**). Attach the circle to the centre of the side of the large cake, positioning it near the board.

2 For the back legs equally divide 4g (⅛oz) of yellow sugarpaste and roll into two small cone shapes (**M**). Attach the legs to the base of the circle.

3 For the front legs take off 3g (⅛oz) of yellow sugarpaste and divide equally, roll into two cone shapes, but slightly longer than the back legs. Attach to the top of the circle coming down between the back legs. Take 1g (⅛oz) of white sugarpaste and roll into four small balls. Press the balls under each foot to make the pads (**M**).

4 For the head take off 8g (¼oz) of yellow sugarpaste and roll into a cone shape. Flatten the top of the cone to form a circle for the head and then shape the trunk by rolling it on the work surface. Make two holes for the eyes, and drop two tiny balls of brown sugarpaste inside (**M**).

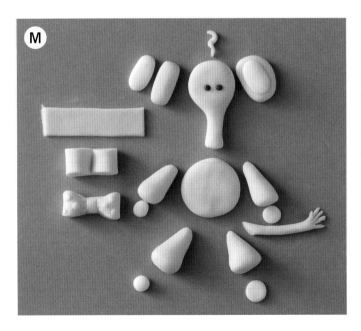

5 For the ears equally divide 4g (⅛oz) of yellow sugarpaste, roll into two small sausage shapes and flatten the shapes with your finger. Make a white lining for each ear using 1g (⅛oz) of white sugarpaste equally divided and rolled into small sausage shapes. Flatten with your finger and then press down on to the ears (**M**).

6 Secure the ears to the side of the head with edible glue. Add a small curl by rolling a thin yellow cone shape (**M**) and attach to the top of the head.

7 For the tail roll 1g (⅛oz) of yellow sugarpaste into a thin sausage shape, marking the ends with tool no.4 to look like fine hair (**N**). Attach to the body.

8 To make the bow roll out 1g (⅛oz) of yellow sugarpaste and cut a strip measuring 8mm (¼in) x 5cm (2in). Apply a line of edible glue across the centre of the strip and fold the ends over to the centre then turn it over and pinch the centre of the bow to narrow in the middle. Using tool no.4, carefully mark the centre of the bow. Add a few tiny dots of white sugarpaste to decorate (**M**), and then attach to the top of the head.

The giraffe

1 To complete the giraffe you will need 35g (1¼oz) of cream sugarpaste and 2g (⅛oz) of dark brown, with a small amount of white. To make the cream colour, mix together 5g (¼oz) of light brown sugarpaste with 5g (¼oz) of yellow and 25g (⅞oz) of white.

2 For the body take off 15g (½oz) of the cream sugarpaste and roll into a cone shape, making a slight curve in the back (**N**). Place the cone on to the cake board, and then push a piece of dry spaghetti down through the centre, leaving 2cm (¾in) showing at the top.

3 For the back legs equally divide 8g (¼oz) of the cream sugarpaste and roll into two cone shapes. Narrow the shapes halfway down, leaving nicely rounded feet (**N**). Attach to the sides of the body.

4 To make the front legs take off 2g (⅛oz) of the cream sugarpaste and roll into a small sausage shape. Make a diagonal cut in the centre, and then attach to the front of the body (**N**).

5 For the tail roll 2g (⅛oz) of the cream sugarpaste into a thin sausage shape, make a diagonal cut at the top and attach to the back. Add a small cone of dark brown sugarpaste to the end and feather it with downward strokes to form the hair (**N**).

6 For the head roll 6g (¼oz) of the cream sugarpaste into a soft cone shape. Narrow the bridge of the nose, leaving a nicely rounded end for the front of the head (**N**). Slip the head over the spaghetti at the top of the body. Mark the nostrils at the front with the end of the spaghetti, and then add a small smile using tool no.11.

7 For the eyes add two small white balls and then roll even smaller brown balls for the pupils (**N**), pressing them on top lightly. Add a white highlight to the eyes with white paste food colour on the end of a cocktail stick.

8 For the ears roll the remainder of the cream sugarpaste into two small cone shapes. Cut a straight edge on the widest end of each cone, leaving the point at the top (**N**). Attach the ears to the sides of the head.

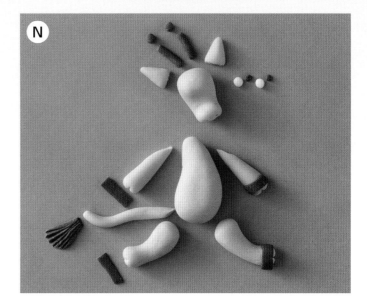

9 To make the hooves roll out 2g (⅛oz) of dark brown sugarpaste and cut four narrow strips. Attach around the base of the legs. Indent the hooves in the centre with tool no.4 (**N**).

10 For the horns add some CMC (Tylose) to the remainder of the brown sugarpaste (see page 9) and roll into a thin lace. Push two very short pieces of dry spaghetti into the centre of the head for support. Cut two short lengths of the brown lace to make the horns, carefully push these over the spaghetti. Add a small ball on the top (**N**).

11 Add the spots to the giraffe using a paintbrush and some buttercup yellow liquid food colour.

The rabbit

1 To complete the rabbit you will need 27g (1oz) of pink sugarpaste and 5g (¼oz) of white. Take off 10g (⅜oz) of pink sugarpaste and roll into a cone shape for the body (**O**), place on to the cake board and then insert a piece of dry spaghetti through the centre of the cone, leaving 2cm (¾in) showing at the top.

2 For the back legs equally divide 5g (¼oz) of pink sugarpaste and roll into two cone shapes. Narrow the lower legs, leaving nice rounded feet. Using tool no.4, cut off the rounded end of each foot leaving a straight edge (**O**).

3 For the front legs roll 2g (⅛oz) of pink sugarpaste into a small sausage. Make a diagonal cut in the centre and attach to each side of the body (**O**).

4 Take 2g (⅛oz) of white sugarpaste, roll into a cone shape and then flatten with your finger. Attach to the front of the rabbit's body. Roll two small balls of white sugarpaste and attach to the feet of the back legs. Mark the paws with tool no.4. Add a small white ball for the tail at the back of the rabbit (**O**).

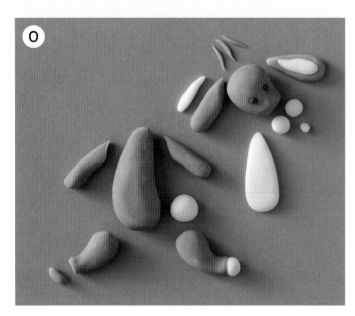

5 For the head roll 6g (¼oz) of pink sugarpaste into a soft cone shape. Flatten the end to form the front of the face. Attach two small balls of white to the front for the cheeks. Mark the mouth using dry spaghetti to make a small hole. Make three thin tapered cone shapes of pink sugarpaste for the strands of hair on top of the head (**O**).

6 For the ears equally divide 4g (⅛oz) of pink sugarpaste, roll into two cone shapes then flatten with your finger. Roll two thin cones of white sugarpaste and attach to the centre of the ears for the lining (**O**). Attach the thinnest end of the cones to the sides of the head, shaping the ears as you do so.

7 For the eyes roll two small balls of white sugarpaste and add tiny dots of dark brown for the pupils (**O**). Add a highlight to each eye with some white paste food colour on the end of a cocktail stick.

A Little More Fun!

Newborn Nibbles

These mini cakes can be made from so many different flavours of sponge, or even fruitcake, using the Silverwood multi-mini pan set for perfect results (see Suppliers, page 126). The flowers and animal toppers are made in the same way as in the main cake, and will delight any younger guests, particularly the baby's older siblings, who will be delighted to take home their very own cake to prolong the happy celebrations.

Christmas Cracker

What a lively table centrepiece this Christmas cracker makes! Father Christmas and his elves are speeding on their way to deliver all the toys. The design is full of fun and captures the very essence of the festive season. Children of all ages will be captivated by this cake, especially if you let them help you make it.

"I hope Father Christmas remembers to save a present for me!"

You will need

Sugarpaste

- ★ 1kg 410g (3lb 1¾oz) white
- ★ 305g (10¾oz) red
- ★ 240g (8½oz) mid-brown
- ★ 140g (5oz) green
- ★ 78g (2¾oz) flesh
- ★ 32g (1oz) black
- ★ 10g (⅜oz) brown
- ★ 8g (¼oz) yellow
- ★ 1g (⅛oz) blue
- ★ 1g (⅛oz) pink

Materials

- ★ Four 6cm (2⅜in) round mini cakes
- ★ Buttercream (see page 26)
- ★ 55g (2oz) sugar flower paste (see page 25)
- ★ Dust food colour in light gold, cinnamon and pale pink
- ★ Black liquid food colour
- ★ Orange and brown food colour pens
- ★ Confectioners' glaze
- ★ Clear alcohol
- ★ White vegetable fat (shortening)
- ★ Edible glue (see page 26)
- ★ Non-toxic glue

Equipment

- ★ 40 x 25cm (16 x 10in) cake drum
- ★ 8cm (3⅛in), 6cm (2⅜in), 5cm (2in), 4cm (1½in) and 2cm (¾in) round cutters
- ★ 4cm (1½in), 2.5cm (1in) and 1cm (⅜in) star cutters
- ★ 12mm (½in) and 1cm (⅜in) square cutters
- ★ No.3 piping nozzle
- ★ Red ribbon 15mm (½in) wide x 1m (40in) long
- ★ Basic tool kit (see pages 12–13)

Covering the board and cake . . . .

1 To cover the board roll out 700g (1lb 8⅝oz) of white sugarpaste to an even 3mm (⅛in) thickness. Cover the board in the usual way (see page 30) and trim the edges neatly with a marzipan knife. Edge the board with the ribbon, securing with non-toxic glue. Set aside to dry.

2 To make the cracker shape sandwich together and coat the four mini cakes with the buttercream.

A

3 To cover the cake roll out 500g (1lb 1½oz) of white sugarpaste into a large rectangular shape. Place the cake on top of the sugarpaste and roll until the paste overlaps. Using a marzipan knife, make a straight cut through both thicknesses then remove the excess sugarpaste. Bring the two edges together to make a perfect seam.

4 Trim the ends of the sugarpaste level with the ends of the cake. Using a 6cm (2⅜in) round cutter, cut out two circles and place one on each end to seal the cake (**A**).

Decorating the cracker

1 Roll out 40g (1½oz) of white sugarpaste into a piece measuring 23 x 4cm (9 x 1½in). Divide the piece into four strips, each 1cm (⅜in) wide. Paint the strips with light gold dust food colour mixed with clear alcohol and set aside.

2 Roll out 45g (1½oz) of white sugarpaste, not too thinly, and then roll over the top using a textured rolling pin. Cut out a strip measuring 23 x 7cm (9 x 2¾in) and then divide equally into two strips lengthways.

3 Place a gold strip around each end of the cake and secure with edible glue, trimming the ends neatly underneath the cake. Add the textured strips next, and then add a second gold strip to finish (**A**).

B

Tip

Place the cracker on an uncovered cake board while you are decorating it. Dust the board with icing (confectioners') sugar to prevent the cake from sticking.

4 For the frilled ends of the cracker you will need 55g (2oz) of sugar flower paste rolled out very thinly. Cut out two 8cm (3⅛in) circles and two 5cm (2in) circles. Using a frilling tool, frill around the edges (**B**). Set any remaining sugar flower paste aside for the stars.

5 Decorate the edges of each frill using light gold dust food colour mixed with clear alcohol on a soft paintbrush. Cover the ends of the cake and the centre of each frill with strong edible glue (see tip, left). Place the smaller frills on top of the larger ones and attach to the ends of the cake.

Tip

Mix together sugar flower paste and clear alcohol into a thick paste to make the strong glue. This glue can also be used to attach the cake to the board when completed.

6 For the centre decorations cut out two 4cm (1½in) star shapes from the leftover sugar flower paste, and then using a small 1cm (⅜in) star-shaped cutter, take out the centres. Using tool no.12, mark with stitch marks from the top of each point to the centre. Make small holes using a no.3 piping nozzle as shown (**B**). Glue the stars in the centre of the frills on each end and paint with gold dust as before.

Father Christmas . . . .

1 **To complete the figure** you will need 188g (6⅝oz) of red sugarpaste. Take off 50g (1¾oz) and roll into a cone shape for the body (**C**). Shape the cone so that it has a rounded front and position the cone on the front of the cake, leaning slightly backwards. Push a piece of dry spaghetti through the centre of the cone and into the cake, leaving 2cm (¾in) showing at the top.

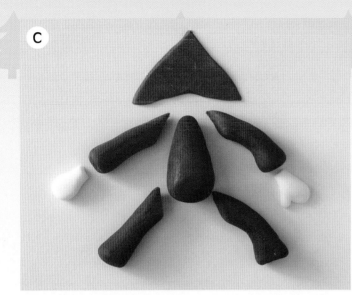

2 **For the legs** roll 46g (1⅝oz) of the red sugarpaste into a sausage shape. Make a diagonal cut in the centre and shape the knee area. Hollow out the end of each leg a little using tool no.3 (**C**). Push a short piece of dry spaghetti into the hip area, apply some edible glue and attach the legs in a bent position.

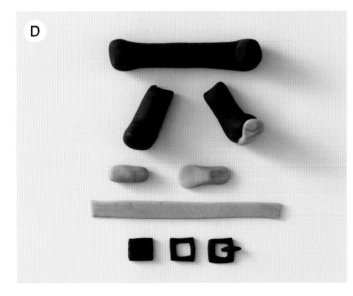

3 **For the boots** roll 25g (⅞oz) of black sugarpaste into a sausage shape. Turn up each end with the flat of your finger, press it forwards to form the foot and make a straight cut in the centre to make two boots (**D**).

4 **For the soles** take 4g (⅛oz) of mid-brown sugarpaste equally divided, roll into two small sausage shapes and flatten to fit the base of the shoes, securing with edible glue. Mark the heels with tool no.4 and make ridges on the soles (**D**). Push short pieces of dry spaghetti into the top of the boots, and then attach with edible glue to the legs. Secure to the side of the cake.

5 **For the coat** roll out 36g (1¼oz) of the red sugarpaste and cut out the shape using the template on page 115 (the template can be adjusted according to the size of your body cone). Apply some edible glue around the body and place the coat at the centre back of the figure, bringing it forwards to meet at the front. Shape the coat to the waistline and let it flow at the back.

6 For the fur trim around the top of the boots and the bottom of the coat, take 50g (1¾oz) of white sugarpaste and soften with white vegetable fat (shortening). Fill the cup of the sugar press (or garlic press) and extrude short strands, cutting them off in clumps using tool no.4. Attach with edible glue.

7 For the belt roll out 4g (⅛oz) of mid-brown sugarpaste and cut into a strip measuring 1 x 17cm (⅜ x 6¾in). Apply some edible glue around the waistline and attach the belt, crossing it over at the front.

8 For the buckle roll out 5g (¼oz) of black sugarpaste and cut out a square using a 12mm (½in) cutter. Cut out the centre with a 1cm (⅜in) square cutter. Attach the shape to the middle of the belt and roll a thin bar to go across the buckle (**D**). Paint the buckle and the boots with confectioners' glaze. For a deep shine add one coat, let it dry and then add a second coat.

9 For the arms first push a short piece of dry spaghetti into the shoulder area. Roll out 28g (1oz) of the red sugarpaste into a sausage shape. Make a diagonal cut in the centre and shape at the elbow (**C**), attach to the body with edible glue. Position the arms so that the left arm is outstretched and the right arm is bent upwards (see tip).

Tip

To keep the right arm in the bent position, push a piece of dry spaghetti down through the wrist area and out at the elbow, connecting it to the leg of the figure.

10 For the gloves take 5g (¼oz) of white sugarpaste and divide equally. Roll into two balls and then make into cone shapes. Mark 'V' shapes for the thumbs, and then separate the thumbs from the rest of the hands. Soften all the edges until smooth (**C**). Make a straight cut at the wrists and attach the hands to the spaghetti at the end of each arm. With his right hand he should be giving the 'thumbs up' sign. The left hand should be in a cupped shape.

11 For the fur trim on the ends of the sleeves, fill the cup of the sugar press (or garlic press) with 10g (⅜oz) of white sugarpaste and extrude short strands as before. Attach with edible glue.

12 For the collar roll a small triangular shape using 15g (½oz) of the red sugarpaste (**C**). Attach the collar around the neck, bringing the ends to the front and leaving a point at the back, then trim with fur made from 12g (½oz) of white sugarpaste as before.

Father Christmas's Coat Template

13 For the head roll 30g (1oz) of flesh-coloured sugarpaste into a smooth ball. Pinch down the neck from the underside of the ball and roll in between your first finger and thumb to make it smooth. Place the ball into the palm of your hand, and with the side of your little finger on the opposite hand, lightly indent the eye area by rocking it backwards and forwards (**E**).

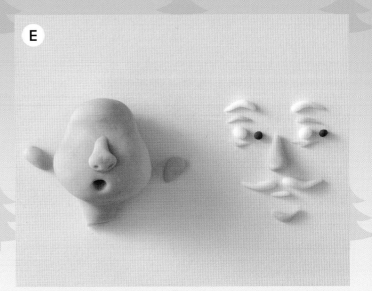

14 Place the head into a flower former to keep the shape. Roll a small cone shape for the nose and glue in the centre of the face, marking two nostrils with tool no.5. Pinch out the cheeks to make them fat and use the end of your paintbrush to make a hole for the mouth, pressing downwards to open it a little as you do so (**E**).

15 For the eyes roll two small balls of white sugarpaste and place just above and on either side of the nose. Press two much smaller balls of blue sugarpaste on top of the white balls (**E**), slightly flattening them with your finger.

16 For the eyelids make two small flesh-coloured banana shapes and place over the top of eyes. Make a second flesh-coloured banana shape and place underneath each eye (**E**). Smooth the eyelids into the face with a soft brush.

17 For the eyebrows roll a small amount of white sugarpaste into two arched shapes and attach over each eye (**E**). Outline the eyes using black liquid food colour and a no.0000 paintbrush.

18 For the ears make two small cone shapes and then attach them to the side of the face level with the centre of the eyes (**E**). Indent the base of the cone with the end of your paintbrush to secure.

19 For the moustache roll two white cone shapes and place underneath the nose (**E**).

20 To make the beard soften 20g (¾oz) of white sugarpaste with white vegetable fat (shortening). Fill the cup of the sugar press (or garlic press) and extrude strands approximately 3cm (1¼in) long. Using tool no.4, slide through the strands taking off a thin layer at a time. Glue to the chin and on either side of the face.

21 Add a second layer of strands to make the beard thicker, and curl the odd strand. Once the beard is completed take three strands, twist them together and place in front of the ears.

22 For the bottom lip roll a small amount of flesh-coloured sugarpaste into a sausage shape and then roll into a point at each end. Curve the shape and attach to the mouth. Attach a tiny rectangle of white to the lip for the teeth (**E**).

23 To make the hat roll 13g (½oz) of the red sugarpaste into a long cone shape. Shape the narrow end into a curved point and hollow out at the fat end with your fingers until it is large enough to fit the head (**F**). Push a short piece of dry spaghetti into the top of the head, apply some edible glue and attach the hat over the spaghetti.

24 For the fur trim use 12g (½oz) of white sugarpaste and extrude as before. Apply edible glue all around the edge of the hat and attach the clumps of fur (**F**). Push the strands into place with tool no.4.

25 Bring the end of the hat down and secure to the side of the hat. Roll a small ball using 2g (⅛oz) of white sugarpaste and attach to the end of the hat (**F**).

The green elf

1 To complete the figure you will need 79g (2¾oz) of green sugarpaste, 24g (⅞oz) of red, 23g (⅞oz) of flesh and 10g (⅜oz) of mid-brown for the hair. Take off 30g (1oz) of green sugarpaste for the body and roll into a cone shape (**G**). Place the cone behind Father Christmas leaving enough room for the legs. Push a piece of dry spaghetti down through the centre, leaving 2cm (¾in) showing at the top.

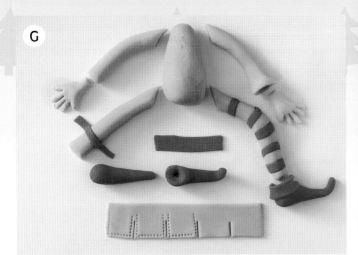

G

2 For the legs take off 25g (⅞oz) of green sugarpaste and roll into a long thin sausage shape. Make a diagonal cut in the centre. To make the red stripes, roll out 4g (⅛oz) of red sugarpaste very thinly, cut out some strips and glue on to the leg neatly (**G**). Once both legs have been covered with stripes, bend the knee area and secure to each side of the body and to the side of the cake. Push a piece of dry spaghetti into both ankles.

3 For the boots equally divide 8g (¼oz) of red sugarpaste. Roll into two cone shapes and taper the ends, curling them upwards. Push tool no.3 into the top of the thickest ends to make a hole. Widen the hole with your fingers. Apply some glue to the top of the boots and slip over the spaghetti at the ankles. Roll out a thin strip of red sugarpaste and glue around the top of each boot (**G**).

4 For the pleated skirt roll out 8g (¼oz) of green sugarpaste and cut out a strip measuring 12 x 2cm (4¾ x ¾in). Make four incisions to form the pleats, and then edge each one with stitch marks using tool no.12 (**G**). Apply some edible glue around the waistline and attach the skirt with the join at the back.

5 For the arms take off 14g (½oz) of green sugarpaste, roll into a sausage shape and make a diagonal cut in the centre. Using tool no.3, push the pointed end into the sleeve to hollow it out and then frill it further with your fingers (**G**). Attach the sleeves to the top of the body, and push a short piece of dry spaghetti into the wrist areas.

6 For the hands equally divide 2g (⅛oz) of flesh-coloured sugarpaste. Make two small cone shapes and flatten the ends with your finger. Using tool no.4, mark the thumbs. Soften the edges and move to one side. Divide the remainder of the hands into two and then into four fingers. Soften the edges of each finger by rolling gently between your finger and thumb (**G**). Mark some fingernails using the end of a piece of dry spaghetti.

7 Slip the hands over the spaghetti at the wrists. Place the right hand on top of Father Christmas's collar and secure with edible glue. Position the left hand on the top of the cake beside the elf.

8 For the collar roll out 2g (⅛oz) of green sugarpaste, and cut out two rectangles measuring 3 x 2cm (1¼ x ¾in). Edge the collar with stitch marks using tool no.12 (**H**). Attach the collar pieces on either side of the spaghetti at the neck.

9 For the buttons roll three balls from 1g (⅛oz) of red sugarpaste, flatten slightly with your finger (**H**) and glue in a line down the front of the body.

10 For the head roll 20g (¾oz) of flesh-coloured sugarpaste into a ball as described for Father Christmas on page 116. Place the head over the spaghetti at the top of the body and turn to look in a backwards direction. Add a small oval shape for the nose and secure to the centre of the face. Using tool no.11, make a smile under the nose and using your paintbrush, pull down the bottom to open the mouth. Add a small dot on either end of the smile using tool no.5 (**H**).

11 For the eyes attach two small white balls just above and on either side of the nose. Press the balls to flatten slightly. Add two tiny blue balls for the pupils looking behind. Add some freckles to the cheeks using an orange food colour pen (**H**). Draw on eyebrows with light brown food colour pen.

Tip

Remember that the balls for the eyes will be larger once you have flattened them, so make them slightly smaller than you need them.

12 For the ears equally divide 1g (⅛oz) of flesh-coloured sugarpaste. Roll into two small cone shapes and flatten (**H**). Attach to the sides of the head, and then indent the base of the ears with the end of your paintbrush to secure.

13 To make the hair soften 10g (⅜oz) of mid-brown sugarpaste with white vegetable fat (shortening). Fill the cup of the sugar press (or garlic press) and extrude the hair. Glue around the head in a thin layer.

14 For the hat use 10g (⅜oz) of red sugarpaste and shape as described for Father Christmas (see page 117) (**H**). Push a short piece of dry spaghetti into the top of the head, apply some edible glue and place the hat on the top.

The red elf

1 To complete this figure you will need 79g (2¾oz) of red sugarpaste, 21g (¾oz) of green, 23g (⅞oz) of flesh and 10g (⅜oz) of brown for the hair. Make the body and legs in red sugarpaste as described for the green elf on page 118 but without the stripes. Position the figure at the back of the cake facing backwards.

2 For the boots use 8g (¼oz) of green sugarpaste, shaping them as before (see page 118). Add a thin lace of red sugarpaste around the boots to decorate them.

3 For the skirt roll out 10g (⅜oz) of red sugarpaste and cut out a 5cm (2in) circle. Take out the centre using a 2cm (¾in) round cutter. Using tool no.4, cut out points around the edge of the skirt (**H**). Slip the circle over the top of the body and arrange around the waistline.

4 Make the arms and hands as described for the green elf on page 118 but using red sugarpaste for the arms instead of green.

5 For the collar, roll out 2g (⅛oz) of green sugarpaste and cut out a 4cm (1½in) circle. Slip the circle over the spaghetti at the neck. Add two green buttons to the front of the body.

6 Make the head as described for the green elf on page 119, but instead of making an oval nose, make it into a cone shape (**H**). The eyes are brown and the cheeks are dusted with pink dust food colour.

7 Make the hair using 10g (⅜oz) of brown sugarpaste in the same way as for the green elf (see page 119).

8 Make the hat using 10g (⅜oz) of green sugarpaste shaped as before (see page 117).

The reindeer

1 To complete the reindeer you will need 79g (2¾oz) of mid-brown sugarpaste and 1g (⅛oz) of red, plus a tiny amount of brown and black for the eyes. Take off 27g (1oz) of mid-brown for the body and roll into a cone shape (**I**).

2 Pull out a short tail at the back of the body. Attach the body to the top of the cake between the two elves, pushing a piece of dry spaghetti down through the centre and into the cake, leaving 2cm (¾in) showing at the top. Using tool no.4, mark the body with some vertical lines to look like hair (**I**). Push a short piece of dry spaghetti into the side of the body to support the legs.

3 For the back legs equally divide 18g (¾oz) of the mid-brown sugarpaste and roll into two fat cone shapes. Narrow the lower half of the cones to form the feet. Using tool no.4, mark the hooves (I). Attach the legs to the spaghetti at the side of the body and to the cake for support.

4 For the front legs take off 10g (⅜oz) of the mid-brown sugarpaste and roll into a sausage shape. Turn up each end to form the feet, and then cut the shape in half. Roll each leg at the other end to taper the shape (I). Attach the legs to the front of the body, marking the hooves as before.

5 Make some chest hair to hide the top of the legs, using 1g (⅛oz) of the mid-brown sugarpaste rolled into a cone shape and flattened. Using the rounded end of tool no.4, mark with downward strokes to make the hair (I). Glue to the front of the body.

6 For the head take 18g (¾oz) of the mid-brown sugarpaste and roll into a fat cone shape. Indent the centre of the shape a little (I). Using a small circle cutter, make a large smile at the front of the head. Using the soft end of your paintbrush, open the lower part of the mouth. Place the head into a flower former while you create the rest of the face.

Tip

When you are placing the pupils in the eyes, think carefully about the direction you want the eyes to be looking in. This can really affect the personality of the character.

7 For the eyes roll two small round balls of brown sugarpaste then add two much smaller black balls for the pupils (see tip). Roll a small banana shape in the mid-brown sugarpaste to make the eyelids and attach with edible glue over each eye (I).

8 For the ears equally divide 1g (⅛oz) of the mid-brown sugarpaste and roll two small cone shapes (I). Secure to the side of the head.

9 For the antlers equally divide 4g (⅛oz) of the mid-brown sugarpaste and roll into two sausage shapes. Curve the shapes around and pinch out three points at each end to form the antlers (I). Push a short piece of dry spaghetti into the top of the head, apply some edible glue and slip the antlers over the top.

10 To finish off the reindeer add three short strands of hair in mid-brown sugarpaste in between the antlers and add a ball of red sugarpaste for the nose (I).

The sack of toys

1 **For the sack** take 100g (3½oz) of mid-brown sugarpaste and roll into a fat cone shape. Hollow out the top of the shape to make an opening at the top (**J**).

2 **For the twisted rope** roll 10g (⅜oz) of the same colour into two thin laces and twist the two together evenly (**J**). Apply some edible glue to the sack and arrange the rope all the way around, with one end resting on the sack, and the other end placed into Father Christmas's hand.

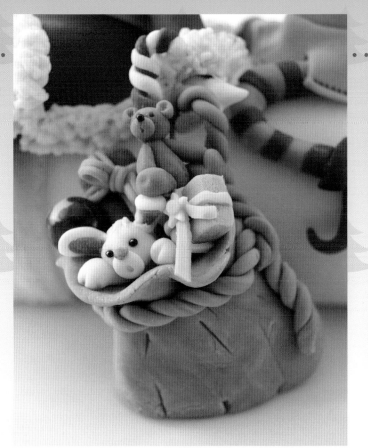

3 **For the green present** roll out 10g (⅜oz) of green sugarpaste to 12mm (½in) thickness, and then cut out a rectangle measuring 3 x 2cm (1¼ x ¾in) (**K**).

4 **For the ribbons** roll out 2g (⅛oz) of yellow sugarpaste very thinly and cut into narrow strips. Attach the strips in a vertical and horizontal position across the present. Make a small tie from a further strip of yellow sugarpaste folded in half and add a 1cm (⅜in) white star shape on the top (**K**).

5 **Make the red present** from 10g (⅜oz) of red sugarpaste cut to the same size as the green present. Make the ribbon from 2g (⅛oz) of green sugarpaste. Run tool no.4 down the centre of the ribbon to mark a line and place across the present in the same manner as before (**K**).

6 **Make the bow** from two short pieces of ribbon folded over to make two loops. Attach the loops on the bow and cut a short piece of the same ribbon to go across the middle to finish (**K**).

7 **For the candy cane** you will need 2g (⅛oz) of red sugarpaste and 2g (⅛oz) of white. Roll a thin lace of each colour and twist the two together. Turn over the top to form the curve (**K**).

8 For the ball roll together a tiny pinch each of red, blue, white and yellow sugarpaste (**K**), and glue to the sack.

9 For the rabbit you will need 5g (¼oz) of white sugarpaste and 1g (⅛oz) of pink. Roll 2g (⅛oz) of white sugarpaste into a cone shape for the head and attach a small ball to the front of the face (**K**). Mark the centre with a line of stitch marks using tool no.12.

10 For the rabbit's ears equally divide 1g (⅛oz) of white sugarpaste and roll into two small cone shapes. Make two very thin cone shapes in pink to line the ears, flatten them slightly with your finger and glue inside the centre of each ear (**K**). Secure the ears to the sides of the head.

11 To finish the rabbit add a tiny ball of pink for the nose and two small black balls for the eyes. Roll the remaining white sugarpaste into a small sausage shape and make a diagonal cut in the centre to make the paws (**K**). Attach the paws to the head and then glue to the sack.

12 To make the teddy bear you will need 3g (⅛oz) of mid-brown sugarpaste. Take off 1g (⅛oz) and divide equally. Roll one portion into a cone shape for the body and roll the other portion into a sausage shape for the legs. Turn up both ends of the sausage shape to make the feet, and then cut in half. Attach the legs to the body (**K**).

13 For the teddy's arms equally divide another 1g (⅛oz) of mid-brown sugarpaste and roll one portion into a sausage shape. Make a diagonal cut in the centre, and attach to the body (**K**).

14 For the teddy's head first push a small piece of dry spaghetti into the top of the body. Roll the second portion into a ball and attach over the spaghetti. Using the remainder of the mid-brown sugarpaste, take off two small balls for the ears and attach to the sides of the head, securing them with tool no.1. Roll another small ball and attach to the front of the face. Mark the centre with stitch marks using tool no.12 (**K**).

15 To finish the teddy add a tiny ball of black sugarpaste for the nose and attach to the top of the snout. Push a piece of dry spaghetti into the mouth area to make a small hole, and do the same for the eyes (**K**). Secure the teddy on top of the presents in the sack.

The cinnamon sticks

1 **To make the cinnamon sticks** roll out 23g (⅞oz) of the mid-brown sugarpaste to a measurement of 9 x 7cm (3½ x 2¾in). Run a line of edible glue along the top edge, roll the paste over to form the stick, and then trim the edge with tool no.4. Make two more sticks (**L**). Dust with a dry brush and some cinnamon dust food colour.

2 **Make the ties** by adding 1g (⅛oz) of white to some leftover mid-brown sugarpaste to lighten the shade. Cut a thin strip and wrap around the three sticks to tie them together (**L**).

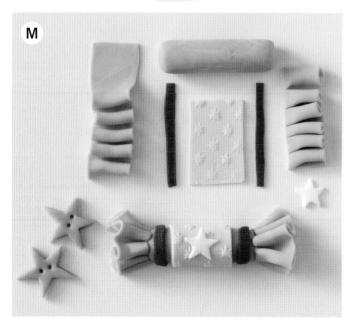

The cracker and cookies

1 **For the cracker** roll 15g (½oz) of green sugarpaste into a short sausage and flatten the ends with your finger (**M**).

2 **To make the frills** at the end of the cracker, roll out 12g (½oz) of green sugarpaste. Cut out a strip measuring 14 x 4cm (5½ x 1½in) and divide lengthways, and then make a frill by pleating the strip. Press along one side of the frill to hold the folds into place. Trim the edges straight, cut in half and attach one frill to each end of the cracker (**M**).

3 Roll out 1g (⅛oz) of red sugarpaste and cut out two thin strips. Place a strip at each end of the cracker next to the frill (**M**).

4 **For the centre decoration** roll out 5g (¼oz) of yellow sugarpaste and roll over with a textured rolling pin. Cut a small piece and glue in the centre of the cracker. Cut out a white star using a 1cm (⅜in) star-shaped cutter and attach to the top of the cracker (**M**). Dust with light gold dust food colour to finish.

5 **For the cookies** roll out 10g (⅜oz) of mid-brown sugarpaste and cut out two shapes using a 2.5cm (1in) star-shaped cutter. Mark with two holes and then dust with cinnamon dust food colour (**M**).

6 **Assemble the completed cake** on the cake board and secure it with strong edible glue (see tip page 113). Place the sack beside Father Christmas and glue the cracker, cinnamon sticks and cookies to the corner of the board.

A Little More Fun!

Perfect Presents

These mini cakes are all wrapped up ready for the party. Square mini cakes made using the Silverwood multi-mini pan set (see Suppliers, page 126) are iced with white sugarpaste and then decorated with large spotty bows. Stars made in the same way as on the main cake are then be pushed into the top for festive cheer. Will there be one left over for Father Christmas? I very much doubt it!

Suppliers

UK

Jane Asher Party Cakes
24 Cale Street, London SW3 3QU
+44 (0) 20 7584 6177
info@janeasher.com
www.jane-asher.co.uk
Sugarcraft supplies

Berisfords Ribbons
PO Box 2, Thomas Street,
Congleton, Cheshire CW12 1EF
+44 (0) 1260 274011
office@berisfords-ribbons.co.uk
www.berisfords-ribbons.co.uk
Ribbons – see website for stockists

The British Sugarcraft Guild
Wellington House, Messeter Place,
London SE9 5DP
+44 (0) 20 8859 6943
nationaloffice@bsguk.org
www.bsguk.org
*Exhibitions, courses,
members' benefits*

Ceefor Cakes
PO Box 443, Leighton Buzzard,
Bedfordshire LU7 1AJ
+44 (0) 1525 375237
info@ceeforcakes.co.uk
www.ceeforcakes.co.uk
*Cake and display boxes,
sugarcraft supplies*

The Craft Company
Unit 6/7 Queens Park, Queensway,
Leamington Spa CV31 3LH
+44 (0) 1926 888507
info@craftcompany.co.uk
www.craftcompany.co.uk
*Boxes, boards, decorations,
edibles, tools and ribbons*

Edible Art
1 Stanhope Close, Grange Estate,
Spennymoor, Co. Durham, DL16 6LZ
Edible sparkles and dusts

Maisie Parrish
Maisie's World, 840 High Lane, Chell,
Stoke on Trent, Staffordshire ST6 6HG
+44 (0) 1782 876090
maisie.parrish@ntlworld.com
www.maisieparrish.com
*Novelty cake decorating, one-to-
one tuition, workshops and demos*

Guy Paul & Co. Ltd
Unit 10 The Business Centre,
Corinium Industrial Estate,
Raans Road, Amersham,
Buckinghamshire HP6 6FB
+44 (0) 1494 432121
sales@guypaul.co.uk
www.guypaul.co.uk
Sugarcraft and bakery supplies

Pinch of Sugar
1256 Leek Road, Abbey Hulton,
Stoke on Trent ST2 8BP
+44 (0) 1782 570557
sales@pinchofsugar.co.uk
www.pinchofsugar.co.uk
*Bakeware, tools, boards and
boxes, sugarcraft supplies, ribbons,
colours, decorations and candles*

Renshaws
Crown Street, Liverpool L8 7RF
+44 (0) 870 870 6954
enquiries@renshaw-nbf.co.uk
www.renshaw-nbf.co.uk
*Caramels, Regalice sugarpastes,
marzipans and compounds*

Alan Silverwood Ltd
Ledsam House, Ledsam Street,
Birmingham B16 8DN
+44 (0) 121 454 3571
sales@alan-silverwood.co.uk
www.alansilverwood.co.uk
Bakeware, multi-mini cake pans

Squires Group
Squires House, 3 Waverley Lane,
Farnham, Surrey GU9 8BB
+44 (0) 1252 711749
info@squires-group.co.uk
www.squires-shop.com
*Bakeware, tools, boards, sugarcraft
supplies, ribbons, edible gold and
silver leaf, decorations and candles*

USA

All In One Bake Shop
8566 Research Blvd, Austin, TX 78758
+1 512 371 3401
info@allinonebakeshop.com
www.allinonebakeshop.com
*Cake making and
decorating supplies*

Beryl Cake Decorating Supplies
PO Box 1584 N. Springfield, VA 22151
+1 800 488 2749
beryls@beryls.com
www.beryls.com
*Cake decorating and
pastry supplies*

Caljava International School of
Cake Decorating and Sugar Craft
19519 Business Center Drive,
Northridge, CA 91324
+1 818 718 2707
criselda@caljavaonline.com
www.cakevisions.com
Flowers and other decorations

European Cake Gallery
844 North Crowley Road,
Crowley, TX 76036
+1 817 297 2240
info@thesugarart.com
www.europeancakegallery.us
www.thesugarart.com
Cake and sugarcraft supplies

Global Sugar Art
7 Plattsburgh Plaza,
Plattsburgh, NY 12901
+1 800 420 6088
info@globalsugarart.com
www.globalsugarart.com
Everything sugarcraft

Wilton School of Cake
Decorating and Confectionery Art
7511 Lemont Road, Darien, IL 60561
+1 630 985 6077
wiltonschool@wilton.com
www.wilton.com
*Bakeware and cake decorating
supplies, tuition*

BRAZIL

Boloarte
Rue Enes De Souza, 35 – Tijuca,
Rio De Janeiro RJ – CEP 20521 – 210
+55 (21) 2571 2242/2317 9231
cursos@boloarte.com.br
www.boloarte.com.br
*Cake decorating, sugarcraft
supplies and events*

NETHERLANDS

Planet Cake
Zuidplein 117, 3083 CN,
Rotterdam
+31 (0) 10 290 9130
info@cake.nl www.cake.nl
Cake making/decorating supplies

GERMANY

Staedter GambH
Am Kreuzweg 1 .D35469
Allendorf/Lda.
+ 49 6407 4034 1000
info@staedter.de
www.staedter.de
*Bakeware, tools, decorations
and accessories*

AUSTRALIA

Planet Cake
106 Beattie Street,
Balmain, NSW 2041
+61 (2) 9810 3843
info@planetcake.com.au
www.planetcake.com.au
*Cake making and
decorating supplies*

About the Author

*Maisie Parrish is often told she has magic hands, and when she begins
to work something magical does indeed happen …*

Maisie is completely self-taught and her cute and colourful characters have a
unique quality that is instantly recognizable and much copied. Over the last few
years, she has been very busy travelling to many different countries, teaching
and demonstrating her skills. She was honoured to be the prime demonstrator
for the New Zealand Cake Guild, and became an honourary member of the
Victoria Cake Guild in Australia. She is a tutor at The Wilton School of Cake
Decorating in Chicago, The International School of Confectionery Education
in New York, Caljava International School of Cake Decorating in California and
Squires Kitchen International School of Sugarcraft in England to mention a few.
She is also an accredited demonstrator for the British Sugarcraft Guild.

Her fans travel thousands of miles to visit her home studio in
Stoke on Trent, England, for a chance to be taught by the master.
People find it difficult to believe that she never actually bakes cakes
for anyone, she considers herself to be a sugar artist who can visit
as many as three countries in a month.

Maisie has enjoyed several television appearances, including *The Good
Food Show* and *QVC*, and she is the author of eight books, with more titles
in the pipeline. Further examples of her work can be seen on her website,
www.maisieparrish.com where she welcomes you into **Maisie's World**.

Acknowledgments

My grateful thanks go to Renshaws for supplying me with a wonderful range of their ready-made sugarpastes – with so many beautiful colours in their range, it has helped to make this book outstanding. Thanks also to Jennifer Fox-Proverbs, Victoria Marks and the team at David & Charles who have given me so much encouragement and professional help in the making of this book. A special thanks to Ame Verso who has done so much work on the editing side, and of course the photographers Simon Whitmore and Karl Adamson. Thanks also to Alan Culpitt for website design services, www.culpitt.co.uk.

Index